CW00430456

The Random Book of…

MATTHEW

Paul Geraghty

The Random Book of…

MATTHEW

Well, I didn't know that!

All statistics, facts and figures are correct as of March 31st 2009.

© Paul Geraghty
Paul Geraghty has asserted his rights in accordance with the
Copyright, Designs and Patents Act 1988 to be identified
as the author of this work.

Published By:

Stripe Publishing Ltd
First Floor, 3 St. Georges Place, Brighton, BN1 4GA

Email: info@stripepublishing.co.uk
Web: www.stripepublishing.co.uk

First published 2009

A catalogue record for this book is available from the British Library.

10-digit ISBN: 1-907158-06-5
13-digit ISBN: 978-1-907158-06-3

Printed and bound by Gutenberg Press Ltd., Malta.

Editor: Dan Tester
Illustrations: Jonathan Pugh (www.pughcartoons.co.uk)
Typesetting: Andrew Searle
Cover: Andy Heath

To Chico

Paul Geraghty – March 2009

Introduction

Matthews are certainly curious creatures. For the most part their historical record is one of miserable failure to achieve anything worthwhile, unless you consider religious fanaticism to be something worthwhile.

There are a few gleaming exceptions in this tragic tale of non-achievement, however: Matthews who made the great human cesspool a little less noisome than it was before.

In recent times, Matthews also seem to have proliferated tremendously, giving us all reason to hope for a bumper crop of Matthew-centric achievement in the near future.

One day a Matthew will reach space. One day a Matthew will win a Nobel. And, yes, one day a Matthew will reign as British Prime Minister, ruling over us all.

Dare I say it, but perhaps one day one of the innumerable actor Matthews might even win an Oscar for his thespian craft.

But, no. That's probably a bit too far-fetched. Let's keep it real, after all.

Paul Geraghty – March 2009

WHAT'S IN A NAME?

The name Matthew is Hebraic in origin, deriving from the word mattīthyāh, which means 'gift of God'. The Latin name Matthaeus and the Greek names Matthaios and Matthias all stem from it.

It has great ecclesiastical significance because it was the name attributed to the author of one of the Gospels, which form the foundation of the Christian faith.

Matthew has generally not been a popular name historically, only coming into fairly widespread use within the last few decades.

Variants of the name include: Mathew, Matt and Matty.

Matthew and its derivatives, such as Matthews, Mathew, Matthewson and Mathieson, are also very common as surnames.

Foreign cognates of the name include:

Armenian: Մատթէոս (Mathios)
Azeri: Matta, Mətta
Belarusian: Мацей (Maciej)
Bulgarian: Матей (Matey)
Catalan: Mateu
Croatian: Matej, Mate, Matija, Matko
Czech: Matěj, Matouš
Danish: Mads, Mattæus, Mathias
Dutch: Matthijs, Mathijs, Mattijs, Mattheus
Estonian: Madis, Mati

Finnish: Matias, Matti
French: Mathieu, Matheu, Matthieu; Mathias, Matthias; Mathis, Matthis
Gaelic: Maitias
German: Mathias, Matthias, Matthäus
Hawaiian: Makaio, Mataio
Hungarian: Máté, Mátyás
Icelandic: Matthías
Irish: Maitiú
Italian: Matteo, Mattia
Latvian: Metjū, Matiass
Lithuanian: Matas, Motiejus
Malay: Matius
Malayalam: Mathai, Matthai, Mathew, Maatthu, Maathan
Norwegian, Swedish, Finnish: Matteus
Polish: Mateusz, Maciej
Portuguese: Mateus, Matias
Quenya: Eruanno, Erunno
Romanian: Matei
Russian: Матвей
Slovak: Matej, Matúš
Slovenian: Matej, Matevž, Matjaž, Matija
Spanish: Mateo, Matheu
Swedish: Mattias, Mathias, Mats, Mattis
Turkish: Matta, Mattayıs

"It was a very simple team talk. All I used to say was: 'Whenever possible, give the ball to George [Best].'"
Sir Matt Busby

———⟫◆⟪———

MYSTIC MATTHEWS

Matthew Parker was the Archbishop of Canterbury during the reign of Queen Elizabeth I. The Church of England was still in its infancy then, with constant disputes about how far it should depart from Catholic tradition. One of Parker's chief concerns was to demonstrate that the Church of England was not, as its critics alleged, a made-up religion, called into being just so that a horny Henry VIII could have his evil way with Anne Boleyn. Parker aimed to demonstrate that, in fact, it had historical roots stretching back into the mists of time. To this end, he assembled a vast library of musty old tomes which he claimed proved his point.

Parker also arranged a translation of the Bible, known today as the Bishops' Version, which was in widespread use until the King James version came to replace it. He even chose to handle part of the translation himself, including, appropriately enough, the Book of Matthew.

A Cat Stevens number

The first song on Cat Stevens' debut album, Matthew &
Son, was a bit of barbed social commentary on a business
which worked its employees too hard.

Up at eight, you can't be late
For Matthew & son, he won't wait.
Watch them run down to platform one
And the eight-thirty train to Matthew & son

Matthew & son, the work's never done, there's always
something new.
The files in your head, you take them to bed, you're never
ever through.
And they've been working all day, all day, all day!

BEHIND THE CAMERA

Matthew Vaughn (b. 1971) is a young British film-maker who first made a name, and a few million quid, for himself by producing two of the best Cockney gangster flicks, *Lock, Stock and Two Smoking Barrels* and *Snatch*.

Later Vaughn stepped up to directorial duties himself on the similarly-themed *Layer Cake*, starring about-to-be James Bond, Daniel Craig. As well as his success in the film world, Vaughn has done not bad in the marriage stakes, bagging German supermodel Claudia Schiffer.

Matthew grew up believing that he was the son of actor Robert Vaughn, but discovered at the age of 31 that this was not true, and that his real father was a British aristocrat called George de Vere Drummond.

Religious Matthews

The **Gospel of Matthew** is one of the core texts of the Christian religion. Despite its name, most modern scholars do not believe it could have been written by the Matthew who is said to have been one of the disciples of Jesus. They base this view on the fact that the Gospels were first written in Greek, while Jesus' followers were mostly uneducated peasants who spoke Aramaic.

Like all of the other Gospels, it was written in the third person, even when the events concerned its supposed author. Most scholars believe that the tradition of attributing authorship of the Gospel texts to some of Jesus' disciples began in the 2nd century AD. Most Christian Churches still officially maintain this view.

Matthew, or Saint Matthew the Evangelist as he is known in some Christian Churches, is thought to have been a tax collector before receiving the call from Jesus. For this reason he is considered the patron saint of bankers and accountants. Matthew is generally held to have been the person referred to as "Levi" in the Gospels of Mark and Luke.

What happened to him after Christ's Crucifixion is not known, although some traditions say he performed missionary work in either Ethiopia or Persia. The relics of St. Matthew were said to have been stored in Ethiopia for a time before being brought to Italy in the 11th century.

Today, purported relics of St. Matthew are scattered all over the world. There is one, for example, at St. Matthew's Church in Westminster.

The Gospel of Matthew is believed to have been written around 30-60 years after Jesus' death, most likely compiled from oral traditions. Among its distinctive features is its emphasis on the Jewishness of Jesus.

It begins with a long genealogy, tracing Jesus' descent from Jewish kings through his father Joseph (although, as some cynics have pointed out, this doesn't actually make sense because God, not Joseph, was said to have been the father of Jesus via the Immaculate Conception).

One key quote from the Gospel of Matthew has been used to preach submission to authority through the ages: "Give to Caesar what is Caesar's."

Matthew Fox was a Catholic theologian whose evolving spiritual views got him kicked out of the Catholic Church in 1988 by Cardinal Joseph Ratzinger, who is now Pope Benedict XVI. Fox transformed himself into a New Age guru, preaching the need for a new Reformation to harmonise Christianity with shamanistic-style nature-based religions.

His views have been set forth in a number of books, including the splendidly titled *The Coming of the Cosmic Christ*, as well as in 95 theses which, in imitation of Martin Luther, he nailed to a church door in Wittenberg while on a visit to Germany.

Fox founded the University of Creation Spirituality in Oakland, California after being removed from his teaching position at the nearby Holy Names College. He has proved an extremely controversial figure within the world of American Christianity, where some, after applying various kinds of numerological analyses and transformations to his name, came up with the number 666 and proclaimed that he was the Antichrist!

Fox's birth name was Timothy James. He adopted the name Matthew Fox on entering the Dominican order, and retained it even after he was thrown out of the Catholic Church. Among his innovative doctrines are that mankind has an Original Blessing instead of an Original Sin.

⟹◈⟸

"It is a sign that your reputation is small and sinking if your own tongue must praise you"
Sir Matthew Hale

A Royal Matthew?

Would you like to see a Matthew ascend to the British throne? It may yet happen…

There is a **Matthew Liddell-Grainger** (b. 2003) in the Royal Family's line of succession. Unfortunately, he is in 330th place, so we'd probably need a few nuclear wars, plagues, catastrophic climate events, major terrorist attacks, the invasion of Earth by hostile extra-terrestrial forces and a few well-placed asteroid strikes before it has any chance of becoming reality.

But you never know. Fingers crossed.

ARTISTIC MATTHEWS

Caravaggio is one of history's greatest artists. Several of his finest works depict scenes from the life of St. Matthew.

Caravaggio's style was blunt and bracing. It introduced a note of realism into Italian art which had never been seen before. Even revered religious figures he sometimes depicted as if they were ordinary bewildered human beings. One of his St. Matthew commissions, a painting called *Saint Matthew and the Angel*, was in that vein.

It had been ordered by the San Luigi dei Francesi church in Rome in 1602. When complete, it showed Matthew working on the text of the Gospel with an angel standing next to him, looking on approvingly.

St. Matthew was depicted as a rough-looking journeyman, however; he was shown as bald, sitting bare-footed at his desk, with his stubby foot jutting gracelessly out into the picture. It was a startling image, but one with a little too much realism for the church. They rejected the work.

Still hoping to satisfy them, Caravaggio produced the *Inspiration of St. Matthew*, another extraordinary work but one which portrayed Matthew in a more conventionally reverential style. This was accepted. The rejected work went to a private collection, and thence found its way to Berlin, where it was destroyed in World War II.

MATTHEW AUTHORS

Matthew Tindal (1657-1733) was an English author whose works played a key role in the development of the religious outlook known as deism. Deism can be seen as one of the first fruits of religion's skirmishing with science. Although it retained a belief in the Supreme Being, and the duty of obeying a moral code, it rejected the outward forms of established religion, and spurned both the authority of the Bible and the idea of religious revelation generally, holding that God's will should be discoverable through the power of reason alone.

Among the elements of conventional Christianity which deism rejected were: an interventionist God, miracles, ceremonies and places of worship.

Tindal himself was raised in the Church of England but later embraced Catholicism, only to reject it in turn as unsatisfying.

Although he rejoined the Church of England, his mind began to wander in other directions. Eventually his beliefs evolved towards deism and he expressed his views in concrete form in the book *Christianity As Old As The Creation*, which came to be regarded as the bible of deism.

Tindal's work was highly controversial in its day. In fact, at one stage his books were burned by order of Parliament!

Matthew Paris (c. 1200-1259) was one of the most celebrated of medieval chroniclers. Like most authors of medieval histories, Paris was a monk. He lived in the Benedictine abbey of St. Albans, a Cistercian abbey in the south of England.

A typical medieval chronicle would contain as much fabulation as fact, with legend and history shamelessly intermingled, and enough outright fabrication to put our modern tabloids to shame. Paris displayed a more scrupulous concern for historical accuracy than most of his peers, however, often appending source documents to his own text.

Paris collected gossip from many of the notable public figures of his day, including royals, who passed through his abbey and with whom he became acquainted.

As well as authoring works in both verse and prose, in Latin and in Anglo-Norman, Paris was an exceptionally talented artist and produced illustrations to accompany the text of his books.

THE HEALING HANDS OF MATTHEW

Matthew Manning (b. 1955) is a kind of British Uri Geller. Strange things first began to happen to him in his teenage years, when a mischievous poltergeist persisted in re-decorating and re-arranging the family home when no one else was looking.

Later, the troublesome spirit followed Matthew to school, where it caused similar disturbances, this time in front of a class full of witnesses. Teachers became so distressed by these events that they considered expelling the unfortunate boy altogether.

As he grew towards adulthood, Matthew found he had some extraordinary abilities. He could see auras around people, for example, and do what is called "automatic writing" or "automatic drawing" in which he would put pen to paper and produce writings or drawings in the style of someone else, even famous artists!

Later on, Matthew discovered he had the ability to heal. Unlike many other people who lay claim to extraordinary powers, Matthew Manning has not shied away from exposing himself to the scrutiny of science. He has allowed his abilities to be rigorously tested under laboratory conditions by a number of respected scientists. In these experiments, Matthew has shown himself able to kill cancer cells and retard the growth rates of cancer using the power of thought alone.

Today, Matthew offers his services as a healer to the general public. He has been consulted by such notables as Prince Philip, Van Morrison, Maureen Lipman, Pope Paul VI and John Cleese.

———⬥———

"Spend 10 minutes collecting everything you need to work on a problem, and unplug the internet for 2 hours. You'll finish in 30 minutes"
Matt Mullenweg, creator of Wordpress

FOOTBALLING MATTHEWS

Born in Guernsey in 1968, Matthew Le Tissier signed for Southampton in 1986, just after leaving school, and remained there until his playing career ended in 2002, scoring 209 goals for the club in total – not bad for a midfielder.

Footballers may kiss their club jerseys, and swear undying loyalty to the fans, but those same fans know that if that same player gets a seductive offer from a bigger club, he will most likely be gone like a shot. **Matthew Le Tissier** was an exception.

Undoubtedly one of the most gifted footballers of his generation, his commitment to Southampton meant that the daily bread and butter of his footballing career was the avoidance of relegation. This he succeeded in throughout his twenty-year career.

Southampton remained in the top flight, although it was a close call on many occasions. Le Tissier was lauded by the fans as the miracle-worker who would grind out a goal on important occasions, keeping the dream alive.

Le Tissier turned down offers from Chelsea and AC Milan among others. Although his devotion to Southampton earned him devotion from the fans – who nicknamed him "Le God", and still today generally rate him as Southampton's best ever player – his international career undoubtedly suffered as a result. He was picked only nine times for England and scored no goals.

Le Tissier became Southampton's regular penalty taker and missed only one out of the 49 he took for the club.

Stanley Matthews (1915-2000) is one of the true greats of English football. His father was a professional boxer who gave his son physical training from an early age. Stanley preferred football to boxing, however, and made his England debut at the age of 13, in a schoolboy side which defeated Wales 4-1.

He was the first football player ever to be knighted and is so far still the only one to have been knighted while he was still playing. That said, he did play for rather a long time!

Kicking off his career with Stoke City in 1931, he continued playing at the top level until 1965, retiring at the age of 50. Nowadays, when most football players are considered past it at the age of 35, it seems absolutely amazing to think that he could have played for so long.

Matthews spent much of his career at Stoke and as a result he won very few trophies. When word circulated that he was planning to leave the club in 1938, protesters marched outside the ground.

The move was called off. Nine years later, though, after getting over the inconvenience of a World War in which he served in the RAF while continuing to play occasional friendly matches, Matthews finally did move to Blackpool in 1947. There he enjoyed continued success, including a memorable FA Cup Final victory in 1953 which came to be dubbed the "Matthews final".

Matt Busby (1909-1994) was born in Bellshill, a small Lanarkshire mining town which was to be the birthplace of a remarkable number of Scottish footballing legends. After making his professional debut with part-time side Denny Hibs, he was signed by Manchester City and then Liverpool, where he remained until the war threw football into turmoil.

When Busby wound up his playing career, he then came into his own as the manager of Manchester United. Under his stewardship the Reds performed well, finishing runners-up in the league before finally winning it in 1952.

It was then, when faced with the challenge of an ageing team, that Busby made a crucial decision. He would not buy in talent to replace those who were leaving. Instead, he would bring on a number of unknown, untried youngsters. It was a bold move, and one that was utterly vindicated by the young team's astonishing success.

Busby's Babes swept all before them, winning the league title in 1956 and 1957. Then, in 1958, tragedy struck. While returning from an away game in Munich the team's aircraft crashed on the tarmac, killing around half of those inside, including many of the team's stars.

Busby himself was badly burned and hovered between life and death for weeks, receiving the Last Rites several times.

After recovering from his injuries, Busby resumed his managerial duties in the following year, gradually rebuilding the team and steering it to renewed success. This success culminated in 1968 when Manchester United became the first English team to win the European Cup.

Today, Austria are well down the FIFA world rankings list. It was not always so. In the mid-1930s an Austrian "Wunderteam" amazed the world with its exploits, only losing controversially in the quarter finals of the World Cup in 1934 to host nation Italy in a game that was forever after to be dogged by claims of referee bias.

At the heart of the Austrian Wunderteam was **Matthew (Matthias) Sindelar**. Following the 1938 Anschluss, in which the Nazis merged Austria into Germany, renaming it Ostmark in the process, Sindelar was offered the opportunity to play for the new unified national team. It was known that he had no sympathy for the Nazis. He declined. He did agree to play in a final Austria versus Germany match, however, before the two teams were merged into one.

Sindelar scored the only two goals of the match, and some say he appeared to taunt the Nazi officials in the audience. Perhaps that was what sealed his fate. His body – he was 35-years-old – was found ten months later, along with that of his prostitute girlfriend. What happened to him has become one of the great mysteries of Austrian history.

The official explanation was that he died through asphyxiation because of a faulty gas pipeline in the house. Few Austrians believed it, even then. Many think he was murdered by the Nazis because of his refusal to comply with their demands or conform to their ideals.

Others say he and his lover may have opted to commit suicide rather than live under Nazi dictatorship. Today, Matthew Sindelar is still considered Austria's greatest ever footballer, and was voted Austria's sportsman of the century in 1998.

Greatest managers in British football history:

Alex Ferguson
Brian Clough
Bob Paisley
Bill Shankly
Matt Busby
Alf Ramsey
Jock Stein
Arsene Wenger
Bill Nicholson
Jose Mourinho

Source: *The Daily Mail*, March 6th 2009

"Where principle is involved, be deaf to expediency"
Matthew Fontaine Maury

A JOHN DENVER NUMBER

One of John Denver's best songs is called Matthew.

It was written as a memorial to his uncle, who was actually called Dean, who lived with the Denver family while John was growing up and was later killed in a car accident at the age of only 21.

Had an uncle named Matthew
Was his father's only boy
Born just south of Colby, Kansas
Was his mother's pride and joy

Yes, and joy was just the thing that he was raised on
Love was just the way to live and die
Gold was just a windy Kansas wheatfield
Blue, just a Kansas summer sky

All the stories that he told me
Back when I was just a lad
All the memories that he gave me
All the good times that he had

Growin' up a Kansas farmboy
Life was mostly havin' fun
Ridin' on his Daddy's shoulders
Behind a mule beneath the sun

"For the creation of a masterwork of literature two powers must concur, the power of the man and the power of the moment, and the man is not enough without the moment"
Matthew Arnold

SPORTY MATTHEWS

Matt Stevens was born in South Africa and grew up there, before moving to England to study. There, he joined the Bath rugby team and soon caught the attention of the England selectors. (His English father made him eligible for the team.)

He won praise for his performances for both Bath and England, and was picked for the British and Irish Lions tour of New Zealand in 2005. Stevens' career seemed to be progressing well, but unbeknownst to his fans, he had picked up a secret addiction to cocaine.

With random drugs tests being the norm for professional sport these days, Stevens knew it was only a matter of time before he was found out. The fateful day came in January 2009. Soon afterwards he found himself banned from rugby for two years.

Matt Hoffman (b. 1972) is one of the stars of BMX sport. Debuting in professional competition at just 15, from the very beginning he achieved extraordinary things, pushing the boundaries of the sport and attempting to turn it into a recognised discipline and, some would say, an art form.

As well as skill on the bike, Hoffman has shown he has a sharp business brain, organising the Bicycle Stunt Series, which quickly established itself as a mainstay of the sport, and starting his own bike manufacturing business under the name of Hoffman Bikes. He has achieved and attempted numerous world records and currently holds the accolade for the highest ever jump.

Hoffman runs a BMX display team which appears at prominent events to try and raise the profile of the sport. Most notably, they performed as part of the initiation ceremonies of the 1996 Olympics in Atlanta.

He has also made a number of film, television and video game appearances, and was involved in the production of the entire series of console games which bears his name.

Matt Morgan's DNA will be preserved in space in case an earthly catastrophe takes out the real Matt. "Who the hell is Matt Morgan?" I hear you ask.

Apparently Matt Morgan is an American professional wrestler who makes regular appearances on the television show *American Gladiators* and his DNA was deemed worthy of preservation thanks to his exceptional physique. Matt's DNA made the trip on 12th October 2008, when Richard Garriot blasted into space aboard a Russian Soyuz rocket.

Garriot was not an astronaut but a videogame designer, and was on board as a space tourist, having coughed up $30 million for the privilege. Garriot decided to use the opportunity of the spaceflight to drum up publicity for his game, Tabula Rasa, a sci-fi **MMORPG** (Massively Multiplayer Online Role-Playing Game) set in a post-apocalyptic Earth.

He announced that he would be taking an "Immortality Drive" into space with him, designed to safeguard precious data in case something bad happened on the planet down below and civilisation was somehow wiped out.

What precious cultural records did he deem worthy of inclusion in this veritable Noah's Ark of knowledge? Er, the saved character data of all the player accounts in his MMORPG. So that's all right then. If you should see a giant asteroid approaching at tremendous speed, you can die serenely, knowing that your level 51 Space Ninja will be safe in orbit up above.

Oh, and he also decided to take DNA data from some notable individuals with him, including the immortal **Matt**.

On 25th August 1875, **Matthew Webb** (b. 1848) became the first man ever to swim the English Channel. He had swum through the night, travelling 39 miles in total, and had remained in the water for 21 hours.

Matthew had always been a strong swimmer, and had always felt great intimacy with the water. While still a child, he had saved his brother from drowning, and, at the age of 12, had signed up to join the crew of a merchant ship. At sea, he had worked his way up to be a ship's captain by the time he became captivated by the tale of an unsuccessful attempt at swimming the English Channel. Suddenly fired with a determination to accomplish the deed himself, he resigned his captain's commission and began a rigorous training regime.

Although his first attempt had to be called off after six hours because of stormy weather, he was not deterred. Two weeks later, he was ready to try again. This time, despite being stung by a jellyfish along the way, he was successful.

The achievement made him one of the great public heroes of Victorian Britain. Unfortunately, tempted by financial considerations, and perhaps enjoying the taste of fame, he chose not to rest on his laurels. He participated in a number of competitive races, and engaged in a series of water-based stunts in return for money.

It was one of these which was to cost him his life. On 24th July 1883, he attempted to swim the rapids at Niagara Falls, but was borne away by the current and drowned. It's worth mentioning that across the generations the Webb family showed a special dedication to the name Matthew. The channel-crossing Matthew's father and grandfather were both called Matthew, and so was his son!

The inscription on his memorial reads: "Nothing great is easy."

ALAS, POOR MATTHEW.

There is only one Matthew in the whole of Shakespeare: Matthew Goffe.

He appears in the second part of *King Henry VI*, and is dispatched by Lord Scales to help subdue an angry mob attacking London.

Matthew isn't much help, however, as the first scene in which he appears begins with the words; "Alarums. MATTHEW GOFFE is slain, and all the rest."

⟹◆⟸

"I could have made money this way, and perhaps amused myself writing code. But I knew that at the end of my career, I would look back on years of building walls to divide people, and feel I had spent my life making the world a worse place"
Richard Matthew Stallman

More religious Matthews

Saint Matthias was the only Apostle not picked by Jesus. He was invited to join the select group when a vacancy was created after Judas topped himself. Mentioned only briefly in the Gospel of Luke, what happened to him afterwards is not known. Some accounts say he went off to preach the Gospel to barbarians and was killed by them. Usually, said barbarians are thought to have been located in Africa, although, bizarrely, there is a plaque in Adjaria, in Georgia, which claims that Matthias died there.

In the 14th century, **Matthew of Cracow** achieved distinction in the field of intellectual inquiry which science-fiction author Robert Heinlein compared to "searching in a dark cellar at midnight for a black cat which isn't there": theology.

As well as being an expert at speculating on how many angels could dance on the head of a pin, Matthew became a professor at Heidelberg University and acted as adviser and diplomat for the Count Palatine of the Rhine, Rupert III, who became King of the Germans.

Matthew of Bassi was a Franciscan monk who believed that some of St. Francis' original vision had been forgotten, and wanted to return to it. To this end he petitioned Pope Clement for permission to wear a distinctive hood which, he claimed, more closely resembled the one worn by Francis of Assisi. Permission was granted and soon other monks wanted to follow Matthew's example.

This led to the founding of a new monastic order which came to be called the Capuchins, after their distinctive garb. They pledged themselves to a life of austerity.

Matthew was elected vicar-general of the order but resigned the position soon afterwards so that he could continue working to spread the faith in his own way, without institutional constraints. The Capuchins were then wracked by political controversy, both internal and external. In the end, to escape it, Matthew of Bassi left the order he had founded. The Capuchins kept going, however, and still exist today. Matthew of Bassi died in Venice in the year 1452.

Matthew of Aquasparta burned in hell despite being a former head of the Franciscan order, a cardinal, an eager advocate of papal rights and the author of numerous theological tracts expounding the glory and majesty of God. The hell he burned in was that described in the Inferno of Dante's *Divine Comedy*. Dante was an opponent of Matthew because the two men belonged to rival factions within the politics of the day.

It was the age of Black and White in Italy, or Guelf and Ghibelline, a kind of Cold War of its day which saw sporadic struggles between the two factions throughout Germany and Italy during the 13th century. In Italy, when one faction triumphed in a particular city it would expel all the members of the other, driving them into a life of exile. This eventually became Dante's fate, and he was naturally bitter about it, immortalising his resentment in beautiful verse.

Matthew was already dead by the time Dante's poem was published, but he perhaps deserved better than to be damned for all time in that way.

OLYMPIC MATTHEWS

Matthew Pinsent is one of Britain's most successful ever Olympic athletes. Rowing first in coxless pairs and then in coxless fours, he managed to win a gold medal at every Olympic Games held between 1992 and 2004, becoming one of only five athletes to win four consecutive golds. His first was achieved while he was still a student at Oxford, and his last was achieved on the verge of retirement at the age of 34.

Since leaving the arena of competitive sport, Matthew has worked as a motivational speaker and as a commentator for the BBC.

Wearing a spiky red Mohican haircut, 23-year-old **Matt Skelhon** from Stilton won a shooting gold for Britain at the Beijing Paralympics in 2008. Amazingly, Matt had only taken up the sport one and a half years before. His talent was immediately apparent and soon he was competing internationally. Matt was not disabled from birth. He was severely injured in a car crash at the age of 20, and forced to use a wheelchair. As his ambition and achievement showed, however, he displayed great resilience in the face of adversity.

Matthew Stockford won three bronze medals for Britain in the Alpine skiing events at the 1992 Winter Paralympic games in Tignes/Albertville. At the next games, held two years later in Lillehammer, he managed to win another

Alpine bronze. Later, Matthew built up a successful property business and became involved in sponsoring Britain's national champion skier, Chemmy Alcott.

Born in California in 1965, the swimmer **Matt Biondi** became one of America's most successful ever Olympic athletes, winning a total of 11 medals in the course of his career. His performances peaked at the Seoul Olympics in 1988, where he won a total of seven medals, equalling the 1972 record of Mark Spitz.

Matching up to Spitz had been Biondi's intention from the start, but Spitz had won seven golds while Biondi fell slightly short of that, winning five golds, one silver and one bronze. In the course of his career, he set a total of 12 world records.

After retiring from competition, Biondi chose to become a maths teacher in California. Amusingly, this has led to constant defacements of his Wikipedia page by disgruntled or mischievous pupils.

One alteration claimed that he had died. Another, by someone who would clearly have benefited more from an English class than a maths class, read "He is well known for his bragging of trophies and awards and likes to talk about his swimming career every second of class."

Matthew Walker (b. 1978) is one of Britain's most successful Paralympic athletes, winning gold, silver and bronze medals in various swimming events at the Sydney games in 2000, a gold in the relay event, as well as two silvers in individual events at the Athens games in 2004. Matthew was first encouraged to take up the sport casually as part of his physiotherapy routine. He found that he was rather good at it, and decided to pursue it competitively.

Matthew Mitcham won the gold medal for Australia at the Beijing 2008 Olympic Games in the 10m Platform Dive. He clinched gold with his very last dive, which became the highest-scoring single dive in Olympic history when it was awarded 112.10 points. It was a nail-biting moment, too, because he needed an unusually high score to beat the Chinese athlete who was just ahead of him at that point.

His gold medal was to be the only one not won by a Chinese athlete in the diving competitions at the games. But Matthew stood out for another reason. Of the more than 11,000 athletes who competed in the summer games, he was the only open homosexual.

After winning the gold, he even ran to hug his boyfriend in the crowd. The fact that he had given up the sport entirely only two years before, and was then persuaded to take it up again, makes his story even more remarkable. Some television stations didn't seem to agree, however.

They offered only minimum coverage of his victory, apparently made uncomfortable by the gay angle. A minor controversy flared about this afterwards and at least one television network offered an apology.

Top 10 British Olympic Legends

1. Steve Redgrave
2. Matthew Pinsent
3. Kelly Holmes
4. Seb Coe
5. Daley Thompson
6. Ben Ainslie
7. Mary Rand
8. David Hemery
9. Linford Christie
10. Don Thompson

Source: *The Sun*, Aug 4th 2008

"An author, whether good or bad, or between both, is an animal whom everybody is privileged to attack: for though all are not able to write books, all conceive themselves able to judge them"
Matthew Gregory Lewis

MATTHEW STAR CURRENCY

Forbes magazine conducts an annual survey to assess the star power of the world's most prominent actors.

Although the methodology is complex – involving close consultation with those in the industry – the end result is supposed to reflect how much "bang for the buck" the actor delivers; in other words, how much difference the presence of the actor makes to the film's commercial success.

Here are the 2008 *Forbes* Star Currency ratings of the world's most prominent acting Matthews.

9)	Matt Damon
55)	Matthew McConnaughey
146)	Matthew Broderick
226)	Matt Dillon
264)	Matthew Fox
376)	Matthew Perry
499)	Matthew Goode
508)	Matthew Modine
656)	Matt Le Blanc
826)	Matthew Lillard
1137)	Matthew Marsden
1154)	Matthew Macfadyen
1298)	Matthew Davis

Source: Forbes.com

"There are certain nights you and your image just aren't in the same bed"
Matthew McConnaughey

<hr />

THESPIAN MATTHEWS

Matthew Marsden (b. 1973) is a British actor who first appeared in the long-running British soaps *Emmerdale Farm*, and then *Coronation Street*. After landing a regular part in the Manchester-based programme, he decided that a life as a British soap star wasn't quite what he was looking for and headed off to America. There he has enjoyed moderate success, appearing in a succession of TV dramas and Hollywood productions.

One of his most notable roles is in the Ridley Scott film *Black Hawk Down*, in which he played Dale Sizemore, the guy who cuts the cast off his arm so he could join his buddies in the fight. This was widely derided as an over-the-top Hollywoodism, but according to the Mark Bowden book on which the film was based, this actually did happen.

Marsden seems to have a bit more in his repertoire than just the ability to pretend to be people he isn't. He holds a black belt in Tae Kwon Do. In fact, his combat prowess is such that the person who trained him for his role in the boxing film, *Shiner*, said that Marsden would even be able to go pro as a boxer!

Matthew has also recorded a number of songs, some of which have charted respectably.

Matthew McConnaughey (b. 1969) has become one of modern Hollywood's most successful actors despite having appeared in no really outstanding films. Critics say he is better known for his good looks than for any notable roles. He works hard to maintain perfect abs and loses no opportunity to take his shirt off and show them off to the world.

For some reason McConnaughey felt it necessary to invent a personal motto for himself. Said motto is "Just Keep Livin" which, like so many of McConnaughey's movies, sails promisingly up towards the inspirational before collapsing catastrophically back into the ludicrous. McConnaughey himself seems extremely pleased with it, however; so pleased, in fact, that he has since festooned his motto over almost everything connected with him, including his production company (JK Livin), his website, a clothes label he set up, even going so far as to brand it into his pet dog's flesh*.

Among his notable extra-curricular activities, in 2007 McConnaughey bravely stepped in and saved the life of a cat which two boys had doused in oil and were about to set alight. Like many Hollywood stars, McConnaughey likes to engage in a bit of do-gooding on the side.

He started a charitable foundation called – you guessed it – JK Livin, to help disadvantaged yoof. Said yoofs don't seem to get much out of the foundation, however, nothing concrete like, you know, a free iPod, or maybe just some food to eat or a shirt to put on their back. All they get, it seems, is inspiration – from McConnaughey. Nice.

*Not really. I made that part up.

Matthew Broderick (b. 1962) is an American actor who retains an eternally boyish aura in the public mind thanks to his success in a number of teenage roles at the very outset of his career. Among these films were *War Games*, in which Broderick played a classic teenage hacker who uses his computer skills to avert global thermonuclear war when a military computer program develops a mind of its own.

Broderick is of mixed Irish and Jewish parentage and, although he considers himself Jewish, retains family ties with the Emerald Isle, which he visits frequently, and where he owns a clifftop holiday home. Despite his affection for the country, the fabled luck of the Irish seems to have eluded Broderick so far.

In his visits to Ireland, he has so far managed to break a collarbone while out horse-riding, and kill a mother and daughter after ploughing into their vehicle while driving on the wrong side of the road. Broderick was tried in connection with the latter incident and pled guilty to a charge of careless driving.

He was fined £100. The light sentence provoked outrage among the victims' family. Although Broderick's acting career eventually fizzled out, he did OK in the marriage stakes, landing Sarah Jessica Parker of *Sex and the City* fame.

"I believe the true line of research lies in the noting and comparison of the smallest details"
Matthew Flinders-Petrie

HOWZAT MATTHEW?!

England cricketers called Matthew:

Matthew Maynard (b. 1966)
Four Test matches played between 1988 and 1994
Wisden Cricketer of the Year 1998

Matthew Hoggard (b. 1976)
67 Test matches played between 2000 and 2008
Wisden Cricketer of the Year 2006
Awarded MBE 2005

Matthew Prior (b. 1982)
15 Test matches played between 2007 and 2009

MORE MATTHEW THESPIANS

Matt Dillon (b. 1964) is a New York bad boy who has carved a 30-year film career out of playing himself in Hollywood movies. Dillon stands in living contradiction of all the patronising advice that teachers and parents have offered to children down through the centuries, telling them they would never get anywhere by playing truant. It was while "dogging it" that Dillon was offered the role that kick-started his career.

Director Jonathan Kaplan was making a film about lawless youth and needed some authentic-looking urchin-types. Dillon seemed to fit the bill. He then reprised the same basic role – of a kid from the wrong side of the tracks – in quite a few films, most notably the Francis Ford Coppola films based on the novels of S.E. Hinton.

Of these, *Rumblefish*, in which Dillon starred along with Mickey Rourke, is a little-known masterpiece, bravely shot entirely in black and white except for the crimson Rumblefish themselves.

Dillon's career somewhat petered out in the first decade of the new millennium, although he did achieve critical acclaim and an Oscar nomination for his role as a racist cop in the 2004 film *Crash*.

You may never have heard of **Matt Moore** (1888-1960), but he is one of only three Matthews ever to make it to the Hollywood Walk of Fame, the famous boulevard strip where only the greatest showbiz stars get to leave their imprint. Matt, in fact, was one of an amazing family of actors, including brothers Joe, Owen and Tom, all of whom were born in Ireland, and all of whom emigrated to the US and enjoyed success in silent movie-era Hollywood.

His sister Mary also enjoyed acting success for a time. During the First World War, however, she volunteered to serve with the Red Cross in France, and died there in the massive influenza epidemic which broke out at the war's end (eventually killing more people than the war itself).

Matt enjoyed the greatest career longevity of any of the acting family, successfully transitioning from silent pictures to talkies and remaining busy in the business until his death. Among his best known films were *Seven Brides for Seven Brothers* and *The Last Time I Saw Paris*.

Matthew (Mathieu) Kassovitz (b. 1967) is one of France's great contemporary cinematic talents. He exploded into public awareness in 1995 with *La Haine*, a fiercely gritty film set in a desolate urban ghetto where disaffected, racial minority youth battle a hostile police force.

Despite being shot cheaply in black and white, the film won a Best Director award for Kassovitz at Cannes, where French police staged a protest against it, complaining about their unfavourable portrayal. The scene was set for a successful career as a film-maker.

As well as directing, Kassovitz has achieved fame with a number of acting roles, most notably Nino Quincampoix in *Amelie*, and Robert, the Mossad toy-maker turned bomb-builder in Stephen Spielberg's masterpiece, *Munich*.

Matt le Blanc (b. 1967) is a heart-throb American actor who, after bumming around for years with small (but sometimes lucrative) parts in music videos and adverts, finally struck it big when he landed the role of Joey Tribbiani in the soon-to-be superhit series *Friends*. When *Friends* came to an end after ten years Matt moved on to the spin-off series *Joey*. Alas, it was less than successful and was cancelled after two seasons.

Matthew Rhys, or Matthew Rhys Evans, is a young Welsh actor who has made a name for himself on television, stage and the silver screen. Matthew, who speaks Welsh, was made a druid at the Welsh National Eisteddfod ceremony in 2000. He plays Welsh poet Dylan Thomas in the film *The Edge of Love*.

Matthew Modine (b. 1959) is an American actor who was raised as a Mormon in Utah but later ditched the religion and moved to New York City to get in touch with his suppressed bohemian side. Much of Modine's early acting career seemed to revolve around the Vietnam War, including parts in the films *Streamers*, *Birdy* and his breakthrough moment as the lead in Stanley Kubrick's Vietnam-era masterpiece *Full Metal Jacket*.

Modine's other notable film credits have included Jonathan Demme's *Married to the Mob*, Robert Altman's *Short Cuts* and Oliver Stone's *Any Given Sunday*. In recent years, he has branched out into directing, without notable success; and political activism, founding the organisations Bicycle for a Day; intended to raise eco-consciousness by getting us all to swap our cars for bikes, and Card Carrying Liberal; an organisation avowedly dedicated to restoring the wholesome original meaning of the word "liberal", before it became a term of abuse in the American political lexicon.

And yes, in case you were wondering, its members really do carry cards.

Matthew Fox (b. 1966) grew up on a remote ranch in Wyoming, which he has described as "the last frontier". Considering the nature of his later success in the television series *Lost*, his childhood contains quite a few ironies. Among these are that his father, a strict disciplinarian, did not allow him to have a television set until he was 15 years old, and that as a child he suffered from aquaphobia, a fear of water.

Fox graduated from Princeton with a degree in economics, did some modelling and turned down a beckoning career as a Wall Street stockbroker before finding his feet in acting. He had prominent roles in the television series *Party of Five* and *Haunted*, before landing his big break when he was cast as Dr. Jack Shephard in the television series *Lost*, in which survivors of a crashed aircraft struggle to survive on, and find a way home from, a mysterious Pacific island.

A depressed spinal surgeon who was escorting his father's coffin back to America, the plot saw Jack rise above his personal difficulties to emerge as the leader of the group of survivors. Fox had originally been intended to appear in the pilot episode only, but his character proved appealing and it was decided to keep him in.

In the end, Jack emerged as the star of the series. Interestingly, Fox had auditioned originally for the part of Sawyer, his great rival as the storyline unfolds.

Matt Damon is an American actor who established himself as one of the top Box Office draws in the first decade of the new millennium. He was voted Sexiest Man Alive by readers of *People* magazine in 2007.

Damon proved he was more than just a pretty face when, with fellow heart-throb Ben Affleck, he penned the script for the 1997 hit *Good Will Hunting*. The film – which tells the story of an uneducated janitor who turns out to be a mathematical genius – went on to win an Oscar for Best Screenplay.

Indeed, it is surely Damon's ability to assess the quality of screenplays, as much as his skills as an actor, which lies behind his ascent to the Hollywood A-List. He has rarely appeared in a bad film and has performed in a great many good ones.

Although Damon had made a name for himself by playing sensitive character parts, he achieved his greatest success in the *Bourne* series of violent action films based loosely on Robert Ludlum's novels.

The Bourne films, which were conceived as a kind of "anti-James Bond," revolutionised the action genre by including meditative storyline elements and bringing action sequences back towards a closer relationship with reality.

HOLLYWOOD WALK OF FAMERS

Matt Moore (1888-1960) is not exactly a household name today. But he is one of only three Matthews ever to make it to the Hollywood Walk of Fame,

The others are Matthew Broderick and Matt Damon.

CRUSADING MATTHEWS

In the 19th century, **Father Theobald Mathew**
embarked on one of the most hopelessly quixotic crusades
ever conceived of by man: to stop the Irish from having a
drink.

Convinced that it was the demon drink which stopped the
poor from ever rising out of their poverty – not lack of
education, an oppressive landlord class, or adverse economic
conditions – Mathew betook himself to signing up those who
would pledge themselves to temperance. He must have been
a powerfully charismatic man because, in this endeavour, he
was bizarrely and extraordinarily successful.

Holding mass rallies all over Ireland, he would deliver his
pitch then sign up tens of thousands at a time. In total,
he managed to sign up an estimated five million people
in Ireland when the total population of the country was
only just over eight million. In the process, he became a
household name throughout the country. Some considered
him a miracle-worker, and almost every Irish village had a
Father Mathew marching band.

If "Apostle of Temperance", as he came to be called, had
kept going, the Irish might be a tee-totalling people today.
Alas, fate threw a spanner in the works in the form of the
Potato Famine, a crushing economic blow which, seemingly
at a stroke, drove the Irish back to the bottle, and laid waste
all his plans.

Matt Cvetic was working in a lowly job as a civil servant
when he got a call from the FBI, asking him to infiltrate
the American Communist party. It was 1943. America
was at war, and Cvetic wanted to do his bit. He had tried
to sign up for the Army, only to be rejected because at
5ft 4ins. he was too short. Cvetic did as he was asked,
burrowing his way into the local Pittsburgh communist
organisation and funnelling information about it to the
FBI.

When Cvetic surfaced in 1949, he appeared before
the House Un-American Activities Committee to give
an account of the inner workings of the Communist
conspiracy. Cvetic quickly graduated to become a celebrity
anti-communist figure. He did radio interviews and a
popular series of newspaper articles told his lurid story.

A film soon followed; a kitsch classic of the McCarthy
era whose title, *I Was a Communist for the FBI*, was its most
memorable feature. For the 1951 release of the film, the
mayor of Pittsburgh organised a parade and proclaimed
Cvetic an American hero. Bizarrely, the film even bagged
an Oscar nomination as best full-length documentary!

The FBI chose to distance itself from Cvetic, however,
feeling that many of his claims about the communist
menace were outlandish and exaggerated. As the 50s
progressed, Cvetic spiralled into personal decline,
receiving electroshock treatment for alcoholism and
eventually dying in 1962.

Matthew of Edessa was a 12th century monk and chronicler whose writings yield important insights into the unfolding history of the Crusades. Most of those who left us with chronicles of the Crusades were involved in one of the major contending factions: the Western Christians, the Byzantines or the Muslims.

Matthew offered an unusual outsider's perspective on events in that he was an Armenian Christian. The Armenian Church had separated from the other major branches of Christianity over theological differences hundreds of years before. Armenian minorities were then spread widely throughout the Middle East, and often not particularly well treated.

Matthew's writings are fiercely opinionated, and he was often roundly critical of his fellow Greek and West European Christians, whose clumsy interventions he blamed for worsening the plight of the Armenians.

In particular, his histories contain a stinging historical rebuke of the Byzantine emperor for having, as he saw it, fatally weakened Armenia, rendering it vulnerable to the Seljuk Turks, and leading ultimately to Byzantine defeat at the battle of Manzikert, which, for Armenians, is one of the signal historical dates, marking the advance of Islam into the former territory of Christendom.

In the 1940s, when anti-communist mania really got going in America, a repentant former communist called **Joseph B. Matthews** (1894-1966), known as "Doc", was at the heart of it.

As chairman of the Dies Committee, Matthews pioneered many of the techniques which would later be taken up by Joe McCarthy himself – such as charges of disloyalty being levelled against people on the basis of their membership of presumed "front organisations" or their casual associations with accused communists – and made infamous under the name of McCarthyism.

As, in 1953, the witch-hunt entered full swing, Matthews was even offered a job as Staff Director in McCarthy's Senate sub-committee. The nomination had to be approved by McCarthy's fellow senators, however, and even in that unsubtle era, Matthews proved a little too extreme for their taste.

Shortly before his nomination came up for the vote, Matthews issued a tract claiming that many of America's Protestant clergy were, in reality, closet communist agents working for Joe Stalin. This sparked outrage even among America's right-wingers. His nomination was not approved.

⋙◆⋘

"I think I'm the first man to sit on top of the world."
Matthew Henson

A Matthew on TV

Matthew Kelly (b. 1950) is a British television show host who first made a name for himself in the show *Game for a Laugh*, which specialised in filming unsuspecting members of the public while subjecting them to contrived and usually unpleasant scenarios.

Kelly also appeared in several other light entertainment shows. Kelly's effeminate mannerisms were part of his act, although the humour of this quickly vanished when in 2003 he was charged with molesting an underage boy.

Although he was later cleared of all charges, Kelly abandoned his television presenting career and entered acting, where he has since won plaudits for his performances.

Matthew Kelly's name entered cockney rhyming slang as a synonym for telly, as in: "What's on the Matthew Kelly tonight?"

MARTYRED MATTHEWS

St. Matthew of Beauvais is one of the martyrs of the
Catholic Church. A resident of Agnetz in northern France,
he had long been noted for his piety. When, in 1099, Pope
Urban II called the First Crusade to do battle with the
Muslims who then ruled the Holy Land, Matthew travelled
with his bishop, Roger of Beauvais, to the Middle East.

When he was captured by the Saracens, he was given the
choice of renouncing his Christian faith or death. He
replied that he would give them an answer on the Friday
of the following week, which happened to be Good Friday.
When that day came, he declared that he had only asked for
the delay so that he could die on the same day as Jesus: "I
give my life to Him that laid his down for mankind". With
that, he was beheaded. His feast day is on March 27th.

Mathew B. Brady was one of the 19th century pioneers
of the art of photography. After learning the techniques
of Samuel B. Morse, Brady went on to found his own
photographic studio. Filled, even then, with a sense that
photographers had a responsibility to preserve the fleeting
moments of history for future generations, he opened
a branch in Washington D.C. to capture images of the
country's great and good.

Among the famous figures whose images are preserved for
us today thanks to Brady's efforts are Abraham Lincoln (for
whom Brady did early campaign work), Ulysses S. Grant
and George Custer.

When the American Civil War broke out, Brady's sense
of mission went into overdrive. He felt he simply had to
record the great events for posterity. Afflicted then by failing
eyesight, he commissioned others to go out into the field
and take photographs of everything that happened.

His 1862 exhibition of images taken on the battlefield of
Antietam brought home the reality of war for the first time
to many of the cosseted urban types who had approved it
and cheered for it. At that time, photographs were not taken
instantaneously. The image had to remain steady for some
time; so, apart from a few posed shots, the photographs
showed mostly corpses.

Brady expended huge sums amassing a collection of Civil
War images. At the war's end, he expected the American
government to reimburse him fully, but in that he was to
be disappointed. Although Congress did eventually offer
him some money, it was not nearly enough to clear his large
debts, and he was forced into bankruptcy. He spent the last
years of his life in obscurity and penury, dying in 1896.

Matthew (Matthias) Erzberger (1875-1921) was one
of the first martyrs to the wave of right-wing revanchist
sentiment which swept Germany in the aftermath of the
First World War, eventually culminating in the rise to power
of Adolf Hitler.

Never much one for the old *furor teutonicus*, Erzberger was a
moderate member of the German parliament who, during
the war, urged Germany to make a reasonable peace while

many of his compatriots were still howling for blood. When Germany's battlefield situation deteriorated, more of his countrymen came round to his way of thinking, and the military duly dispatched him to sign the peace.

After the treaty had been signed, he was forced to argue for its acceptance against strenuous opposition. This made him a hate figure on the German right, and their rancour did not take long to make itself felt. On 26th August 1921, while on holiday in Bad Griesbach, Erzberger was shot dead by two members of the sinister Organisation Consul, a right-wing extremist organisation which carried out many political assassinations during the inter-war years.

Wilhelm II, the former German Kaiser, then living in exile in Holland, had called Erzberger "a personal enemy of my house" and reportedly celebrated when he heard of his death.

In 1998, **Matthew Shepard** was a 21-year-old student at the University of Wyoming. After meeting Aaron James McKinney and Russell Arthur Henderson in a gay bar, he left with them in their car. The two men beat, robbed and tortured him, as they had planned to do all along, taking him to a remote stretch of the countryside and leaving him tied to a fence to die.

Shepard was discovered almost a day later by a passer-by. He was in a coma but still alive. Although he received prompt medical treatment, he never regained consciousness and died a few days later.

The perpetrators were quickly discovered. The case became a cause célèbre in America, receiving widespread coverage in the media and prompting calls for new Hate Crimes legislation to be passed. Matthew's mother, Judy, has become a crusader against anti-gay prejudice.

Matthew Shepard's story proved inspirational to many in the entertainment industry. A film was made about his life and its horrific end. Songs were dedicated to him. Some in-the-closet gays were even moved to "come out" and reveal themselves by the tragic episode. Both of his murderers were each eventually sentenced to two consecutive life terms of imprisonment.

⟫◆⟪

"It is all very well to be able to write books, but can you waggle your ears?"
James Matthew Barrie to H. G. Wells

BOOTIFUL MATTHEW

Bernard Matthews left school at 16 with no qualifications. Despite that, he managed to build up an impressive business empire, marketing turkey to the British public and, later, the rest of the world. The business made him immensely wealthy. Today, he is believed to have a fortune of around £300 million.

Matthews first entered the public eye with a series of television commercials in which he appeared personally, expounding the merits of his turkey products, which, in his thick accent, he proclaimed to be "bootiful, really bootiful".

Said products acquired a slightly less salubrious reputation later on, though, when a series of unfortunate incidents damaged the company image. Secretly recorded film was broadcast nationwide, showing dirty, injured birds living in cramped conditions at one of Matthews' farms.

Celebrity chef Jamie Oliver also denounced one of Matthews' most successful products, the Turkey Twizzler, as one of the blights of the British school dinner scene. Most shockingly, two turkey handlers at one of Matthews' plants were caught playing baseball with live turkeys. One would throw the turkey into the air, while the other would whack it with a giant pole.

GROUNDBREAKING MATTHEWS

Matthew Fontaine Maury (1806-1873) was an American who revolutionised the science of navigation in the age of sail. After joining a ship's crew as a young lad of 16, he learned much about contemporary navigation techniques and became dissatisfied with their limitations. He even penned a treatise on the subject himself, which soon became the standard textbook used for training in the American navy.

Following a leg fracture at the age of 33, which left him with enduring pains, Matthew's career as an active seaman came to an end. He was soon appointed to the post of Superintendent of the US Naval Observatory.

His job was considered an uninspiring bureaucratic backwater, but Matthew used it to achieve extraordinary things. The Observatory served as depository for vast numbers of ships' logs, which vessels were required by law to submit after their voyages.

Matthew and his staff pored over these musty tomes, sifting and comparing, extracting useful little nuggets of information which might help ships' navigators.

The result was Maury's *Winds and Current Charts*, which at first was circulated privately among mariners in return for their help in improving it further.

It contained many tips which a clever navigator could use to speed his ship's voyage. Intended for naval use originally, civilian interest in it was soon piqued when a clipper captain used the book to help slash the record journey time for a voyage from New York to San Francisco round Cape Horn.

Patrick Matthew was a 19th century Scottish landowner who, quite casually, in a book he wrote on the growing of trees to yield naval timber supplies, sketched out the Theory of Evolution 30 years before Charles Darwin published his landmark tome *On the Origin of Species*.

There is no evidence that Darwin had ever read Matthew's book prior to his own publication, and, indeed, he seemed rather flabbergasted when he eventually did read it, confessing to a friend that Matthew "briefly but completely anticipates the theory of Natural Selection".

Darwin later made generous public acknowledgements of Matthew's work in letters to periodicals and in later editions of his work. Matthew himself had calling cards printed, proclaiming himself to be the discoverer of the principle of natural selection. He later wrote to Darwin, insisting that, as an explanation, evolution was not all-encompassing; it could not explain beauty, he believed, leaving room for a Creator.

Matthew was also involved in a number of political initiatives motivated by humanitarian impulses, such as the Chartist movement and plans to address the blight of urban poverty in Dundee.

Commodore **Matthew C. Perry** (1794-1858) was the American naval officer who opened Japan up to Western trade and influence. For centuries, Japan had been a society largely closed to foreigners. Only limited trade with the Chinese and Dutch was permitted through the port of Nagasaki. The Americans had been trying to pry open the Japanese market for some time and had become convinced that success would require a show of force.

As a result, Commodore Perry was dispatched with a letter from US President Millard Fillmore and a suitably impressive fleet of ships. Perry had prepared carefully for his historic mission, reading up on Japanese culture and consulting noted Western Japanologists.

After arriving at Uraga on July 8th 1853, Perry met with local officials. They demanded that he travel to Nagasaki instead and present his petition there. Perry refused, insisting that he be allowed to hand over the President's letter in Uraga and threatening violence if he was not.

Faced with the superior Western technology, the Japanese had no choice but to relent. They accepted the letter which requested the establishment of diplomatic relations.

When the reply came, it was favourable. Americans would henceforth be allowed to trade with Japan and a US Consul would be allowed into the country. Matthew Perry was feted as a hero on his return to his homeland. He died only four years later of cirrhosis of the liver.

Matthew (Matteo) Ricci was an Italian Jesuit priest who became one of the pioneers of Western contact with China. After serving as a missionary in India, and earning a reputation as a master linguist, he was invited to join the Jesuit's China Mission in 1582.

Through artful diplomacy, the Jesuits had gained permission to establish a permanent outpost in Zhaoqing at a time when entry into China was normally forbidden to Westerners. The essence of the Jesuit approach was to blend in, as far as possible, with existing Chinese culture.

To this end, Ricci set about mastering Mandarin and ultimately authored a number of books in it, both translations of important Western texts and original works of his own.

His understanding of Confucianism earned him respect among China's scholarly elite, causing them to take everything else he had to say more seriously than would otherwise have been the case.

Paradoxically, at a time when the Catholic Church in Europe was persecuting Galileo, Ricci's presentation of Western scientific achievements in China aroused great interest, and served as a kind of appetiser for his religious doctrines. Ricci's map of the world was a sensation, and was widely copied. For the first time it gave the Chinese a sense of their place in the wider world.

Small communities of Catholic believers were established in many parts of China as a result of the Jesuit preaching.

Matthew Flinders (1774-1814) was a British sailor who is one of those credited with (or should that be blamed for?) discovering Australia.

He first saw the Terra Australis in a ship commanded by Captain William Bligh, with whom he seemed to get along slightly better than did his previous crew, the infamous *Bounty* mutineers, who had the crazy and utterly reprehensible idea that hanging out on Tahiti drinking coconut oil with a bunch of half-naked hula girls was better than stewing and sweating in close-knit proximity to fifty other rough-hewn males on behalf of King and Country.

Although the land down under had been known about in Europe for almost two centuries, it had never been fully charted. Flinders helped clear up some of the remaining geographical mysteries, such as whether Van Diemen's Land (now Tasmania) was an island.

He also began the systematic study of the continent's curious wildlife, allegedly becoming the first man ever to dissect a wombat, although doubtless many obscure aborigines would have been able to dispute that claim if they had been able to speak English.

Flinders later published a book about Australia in which he expressed a strong preference that it should be called Australia, rather than the then favoured names of Terra Australis or New Holland. His book was widely read and undoubtedly played a key role in causing the British government to adopt the name Australia officially a short time later. In Australia today, innumerable places and institutions are named in Flinders' honour.

Matt Flinders (1853-1942) clearly had questing in his genes because his grandson, who had been named in his honour, also made something of a name for himself as an explorer. While his forebear secured fame exploring Australia, young **Matthew Flinders-Petrie** began with a much higher civilisation: that embodied by the prehistoric monuments of Stonehenge, which happened to be right next door to where he grew up.

Petrie is considered the father of Egyptology – that is serious Egyptology – as opposed to the "I say, old boy, those sand wogs really knew how to build them, eh what?" type of imperial amateurishness which had prevailed before.

He carried out systematic surveys of the ancient monuments and debunked some of the more fanciful theories about their construction then kicking around.

When we consider the popular modern notions that the pyramids and Sphinx were built, not by ancient Egyptians, but by spacemen or some lost Atlantean super-civilisation, Flinders-Petrie's words seem strangely prescient.

"The Great Pyramid has lent its name as a sort of by-word for paradoxes; and, as moths to a candle, so are theorisers attracted to it."

Sir William Matthew Flinders Petrie, *The Pyramids and Temples of Gizeh* 1883

Rather than pie in the sky, Petrie preferred shards on the ground. He became an avid collector of the kind of archaeological artefact his predecessors had contemptuously ignored: broken bits of pottery, which he would assiduously collect and painstakingly catalogue.

———◆———

"We were the only ones interested in comedy. Everybody else wanted to be Martin Scorsese"
Matt Stone, co-creator of *South Park*

MORE CRUSADING MATTHEWS

Matthew Thornton was one of the 56 signers of America's Declaration of Independence from Britain and the only Matthew among them. Born in Ireland in 1714, he migrated with his family first to Maine and then to Massachusetts where he studied and then practised medicine.

He became a respected figure in the community, served as a judge and was active in local politics. In 1768, his family was granted a township which bore their name, Thornton. It still exists today.

As the quarrel between Britain and its disaffected colonials gathered force, Thornton became one of the leaders of the opposition. As royal government broke down, he became the de facto chief of government in New Hampshire.

In this capacity he travelled to Pennsylvania to consult with the Continental Congress, the embryonic American parliament which produced the Declaration of Independence. Although Matthew Thornton was not present when the Declaration was first unveiled, he was allowed to append his name to it later in November of that year.

After the war, Matthew ended his medical practice and settled down to a life of farming and local politics. He also operated a ferry on the Merrimack River. The town which grew up around it is still known as Thornton's Ferry.

Matthew Hopkins was a strict religious puritan whose mania found a bloody outlet in the chaos of civil war England. Styling himself the "Witchfinder-General", Hopkins stalked the parishes of East Anglia, ferreting out new victims.

Bodily torture was banned in England so Hopkins was forced to resort to more subtle methods, such as long sleep deprivation sessions which could last for days.

Hopkins' other favoured "interrogation" technique was perhaps the most diabolical of all:

Tie up the suspect and throw him or her in the river. Any victim who survived had to be a witch because only supernatural powers could have prevented drowning. Dying meant that the suspect was innocent, a verdict that would no doubt have been of great comfort to the unfortunate non-witch in the afterlife.

Hopkins' reign of terror lasted for two years and was brought to an end only by his death through illness in 1647.

Some say he was cursed by one of his victims, who may have been a real witch since her curse seemed to work. Hopkins' life and work were commemorated in the film *Witchfinder-General*, released in 1968.

Judge **William Matthew Byrne Jnr.** became the star of one of most colourful court cases in the 1970s. The so-called Pentagon Papers were a voluminous history of the Vietnam War, originally intended only for internal consumption within America's Department of Defense.

They discussed all matters relating to the war, including coups, assassinations, morally dubious local supporters and policy failures with a brutal frankness.

Daniel Ellsberg was a military analyst employed by the Rand Corporation whose work brought him into contact with the Pentagon Papers. Fascinated, and at the same time appalled, by their contents, he decided the world needed to see them for itself.

He then engaged in the laborious exercise of smuggling the thousands of pages out of his office and photocopying them.

Ellsberg leaked the papers to *The New York Times*, which began publishing extracts from them on a daily basis. When the government took out an injunction to stop the paper from continuing, the *Washington Post* took up the torch and began publishing more extracts. Nixon decided to make an example of Ellsberg, who was charged with conspiracy, espionage and theft.

During the trial, it emerged that not only had the Nixon administration been spying on Ellsberg, but had arranged for his psychologist's office to be broken into so that Ellsberg's file could be read, and the presumably damaging material thus gleaned used to discredit Ellsberg in public!

When the Nixon team's nefarious conduct was revealed, Judge Matthew Byrne decided that the trial could no longer be allowed to continue, declaring that it offended "a sense of justice".

Matthew (Matthias) Rath went from being an ordinary medical researcher at a German institute to a firebrand crusader against the whole panoply of modern medicine. He believes many modern drugs do more harm than good, and that ingesting sufficient quantities of vitamins and minerals can cure many serious diseases.

His supporters hail him as a messiah-like visionary; his detractors call him a crackpot whose ideas are positively dangerous. Rath worked with Nobel prize-winning scientist Linus Pauling who also held highly distinctive views about the possible health effects of vitamins.

After Pauling's death, Rath built up a successful business empire, selling vitamins to the suckers, I mean punters. In 2008, he sued *The Guardian* newspaper in Britain after it published a series of articles about him in its Bad Science column. Rath later dropped the action and was ordered to pay costs.

Since Mr. Rath is known for his litigious habits, let me conclude by saying that he is not a crackpot at all but a genius. Yes, a genius I tell you, a genius!

Matthew N. Fraser became the focus of a celebrated legal case which defined the limits of free speech in American schools in 1983. Fraser was a senior school pupil who was nominating another pupil, Jeff Kuhlman, for a position on the student representative body. The speech he gave was full of sexual innuendoes but was not explicitly obscene. It read as follows:

"I know a man who is firm – he's firm in his pants, he's firm in his shirt, his character is firm – but most of all, his belief in you the students of Bethel, is firm. Jeff Kuhlman is a man who takes his point and pounds it in.

If necessary, he'll take an issue and nail it to the wall. He doesn't attack things in spurts – he drives hard, pushing and pushing until finally – he succeeds. Jeff is a man who will go to the very end – even the climax, for each and every one of you. So please vote for Jeff Kuhlman, as he'll never come between us and the best our school can be."

Fraser was suspended by the school for three days. Angry about what had happened, he took the school to court, arguing that it had wrongly punished him for exercising his right of free speech. He won the case, and a subsequent appeal by the school, but these favourable verdicts were eventually overturned by the Supreme Court which declared that children in a school setting did not have as much free speech as adults did in public.

Richard Matthew Stallman (b. 1953) is one of the doyens of the open-source software movement, or, as he idiosyncratically insists on calling it, the free software movement.

With his core views formed back in the days when computers were the preserve of industry and academe, Stallman observed the rise of the proprietary software model, which was to dominate the mass market, with dismay. He believes in free software with an evangelist's passion.

Others argue that open-source software is superior for practical reasons, because the bugs are more likely to be ironed out when the code is available for public inspection, for example.

Stallman, however, insists on it as a fundamental moral right. His crusade is fundamentally political. Indeed, his no-frills website (www.richardstallman.org) is primarily a list of political calls to arms, and many of his causes have nothing to do with technology.

Stallman is an unpaid research associate at the Massachusetts Institute of Technology and, with his long, flowing hair and beard, gives the impression of being an eternal student, an impression bolstered by the fact that for a long time he had no formal residence but would just fall asleep in his office at MIT.

Stallman is essentially a modernised, high-tech hippy who never got the message that The Man had won, and, like one of the fabled Japanese soldiers on Pacific micro-islands still fighting World War II long after the surrender document had been signed, has continued the Flower Power crusade into the modern age.

———◆———

"I envision a future where there'll be 300 million reporters, where anyone from anywhere can report for any reason. It's freedom of participation absolutely realised"
Matt Drudge

High School massacred Matthews

There have been an inordinate amount of Matthews murdered in schools across North America...

Matthew Kercher was one of the school pupils shot in the library at Columbine High School as Harris and Klebold went on their deadly rampage.

The 16-year-old was a varsity lineman football player, which made him a particularly tempting target for the spree killers, who particularly hated "jocks" – American slang for athletes.

Like most of the others who died in the library, Kercher was unsuccessfully attempting to hide under a table, as he had been instructed to do by a teacher who saw Harris and Klebold coming.

Apparently, there was simply no other way out of the library.

Crazed Korean student Seung-Hui Cho perpetrated America's worst gun massacre at Virginia Polytechnic Institute and State University on April 16th 2007, killing 32 people in total.

Among them were two Matthews:

The 24-year-old **Matthew Gwaltney** was both a student and teacher at Virginia Tech, pursuing post-graduate studies and teaching undergraduate classes at the same time.

A sports enthusiast, he had a bright career ahead of him, with several lucrative job offers from local engineering firms already lined up.

Matthew La Porte, 20, was an Air Force cadet in his first year of studying Politics and Leadership at Virginia Tech when Cho gunned him down. La Porte was a musician who played in the Air Force band and intended to build a career in the military.

⟫⟩◆⟨⟪

MATTHEW, THE HIGH SCHOOL KILLER

On September 23rd 2008, it was the turn of a Matthew to turn perpetrator in a school massacre.

Matti Juhani Saari, a 22-year-old trainee chef, went on a rampage at a vocational college in Kaujahoki, a small town in Finland.

Matthew murdered ten people in total, nine students and a teacher, in a 90-minute killing spree, before shooting himself in the head.

He actually survived his own suicide attempt and was taken to hospital for treatment, but succumbed to his injuries shortly afterwards.

Saari was obsessed with previous school massacres, participating in chat groups on the internet where photos and videos of previous incidents were shared. He also had his own YouTube page, where he had posted a video of himself practising with a pistol.

Bizarrely, police had received an anonymous tip-off about Saari before the massacre took place. They viewed his YouTube video and interviewed him on the day before the killings, but took no action as they believed he had committed no crime.

MATTHEW WILLIAMS

Matt Williams (USA)
bassist in the band He Is Legend

Matt Williams (USA)
Major League Baseball player

Matthew Williams (Wales)
footballer

Matt Williams (USA)
Texas Tech Red Raiders (American Football)

Matt Williams (Australia)
Rugby Union coach

Matt Williams (USA)
television producer; *Roseanne* and *Home Improvement*

Matt Williams (USA)
former Major League Baseball player (right-handed pitcher)

Matt Williams (USA)
former Major League Baseball player (left-handed pitcher)

Matt Williams (Australia)
show jumper

More groundbreaking Matthews

Matthew Baillie was a Scottish physician who has been called "the father of modern pathology". He came from a distinguished family, his father being a professor of divinity at Glasgow University and his mother the sister of the eminent anatomists John and William Hunter; his sister was the noted poet and dramatist Joanna Baillie.

Against the wishes of his father, who wished to see him pursue a career in divinity too, Matthew moved to London to study anatomy under William Hunter. He earned a medical degree from Oxford in 1789 and four years later published the first ever book on pathology, *The Morbid Anatomy of Some of the Most Important Parts of the Human Body* (1793).

With his sharp intellect, and the experience gained from innumerable pathological examinations, he was able to arrive at several novel medical insights.

In the latter half of his life, Matthew gave up writing and focused on his private medical practice. He became physician extraordinary to King George III and tended him in his final illness.

This royal connection led to him being offered a baronetcy, but he declined it. He did accept another honour, however, the fabled gold-headed cane which for generations had been carried by Britain's most distinguished clinicians. Matthew Baillie was its fifth recipient. After his death in 1823, aged 61, the cane came to be displayed like a sacred relic at the New College of Physicians in London.

Matthew Henson (1866-1955) was a celebrated black American explorer. At the age of six, he left his home in Maryland to join a ship as a cabin boy. There a kindly captain took him under his wing and taught Matthew to read and write.

When the captain died, Matthew was recruited as a valet by the future admiral, then a mere lieutenant, Robert Peary. Peary was determined to make a name for himself through exploration, and soon hit on the idea of Arctic adventures.

Peary and his faithful sidekick Matthew Henson lived among the Inuit people, learning about their way of life and the techniques they had developed to cope with the harsh environment they lived in.

When Peary and Henson made a bid to become the first adventurers ever to reach the North Pole, what they had learned from the Inuit proved invaluable. Henson acted as the trailblazer for the expedition, walking out ahead of the other men.

Thus it was he who first reached the North Pole, or so it appeared, on April 6th 1909. The team soon returned to civilisation to boast about their achievements. Unfortunately, Frederick Cook claimed to have reached the North Pole at about the same time.

These competing claims gave rise to a long running controversy. At the time, the American National Geographic Association adjudicated the matter and decided that the Peary-Henson team's claim should be accepted.

Peary was feted as a great man and became a national hero. Matthew Henson, however, was barely recognised at all, even though Peary described him as the single indispensable member of the team. A black man in a still deeply racist America, Henson remained for long an obscure figure.

Matthew Boulton (1728-1809) was a Birmingham industrialist whose family had a long history of metalworking craftsmanship. When he hooked up with James Watt, inventor of the steam engine, he was able to put his knowledge to use, forming a partnership which played a key role in instigating what would come to be called the Industrial Revolution.

Together they produced hundreds of steam engines which were soon in use across the length and breadth of Britain, galvanising the new age.

Boulton was the very opposite of the uncouth capitalist pig of caricature, consistently demonstrating both profound humanitarian concern and an interest in matters cultural.

He maintained a pioneering social insurance scheme for his workers, under which they would pay a small percentage of their earnings in return for which either they or their families would receive generous treatment in case of illness, accident or fatality. Boulton built a theatre in Birmingham and became a fellow of the Royal Society.

With other northern luminaries, he was also a member of the Lunar Society which at that time played a key role in stimulating intellectual developments in Britain.

British Columbia was one of the last parts of North America to be settled by European immigrants. As late as 1850, its white population could be numbered in the hundreds. In 1858, it was proclaimed a British colony and a handful of men set out to bring order and prosperity to the territory.

One of the most remarkable of these pioneers of British Columbia was **Matthew Baillie Begbie** (b. 1819), who was appointed a judge in the province. A Cambridge-educated barrister, he helped bring law to the lawless, acquiring a reputation as someone who was always fair to the marginal and excluded, including the aboriginal inhabitants, whose native languages he mastered.

In 1871, British Columbia joined the Canadian Confederation, and Begbie was appointed the province's first Chief Justice. On a brief return to Britain in 1875, Begbie was knighted at Balmoral.

You've heard of Christopher Columbus, the Italian working for the King of Spain who "discovered" America even though there were people already living there and the Vikings had "discovered" it in similar fashion hundreds of years before. Well, England's King Henry VII had a slightly more hapless Italian explorer of his own: John Cabot.

After an abortive 1496 mission in which his crew rebelled against him, he set off again the next year in his 18-man schooner, **The Matthew**, which had been named after his wife Mattea.

Cabot was looking for a quick route to Asia and thought he had found it. In fact, what he had found was Canada, specifically Newfoundland, the island off Canada's southern seaboard which is famous today for, er, fish and jokes about people from Newfoundland (which are a bit like Irish jokes in Britain).

Although the exact location of his landfall is in dispute among scholars, the British and Canadian governments say it was at Cape Bonavista. After a few weeks spent exploring the surrounding region, Cabot returned to England to be greeted as a hero.

He was showered with every kind of honour imaginable and the next year set off once again to resume his explorations. He was never heard from again. He and his whole fleet, including *The Matthew*, are presumed to have been lost at sea.

To commemorate the 500th anniversary of Cabot's historic voyage, the city of Bristol commissioned a replica of his ship, *The Matthew*, to be built. It successfully recreated the original journey to Newfoundland with a crew of 18. Today it sits in Bristol harbour, receiving visitors and taking them out for excursions on the water.

"*Every time a Conservative crosses the floor to join Labour, there is a small but measurable increase in the average IQ of both parliamentary parties*"
Matthew Parris

KEEP THEM PEELED MATTHEW

Matthew Amroliwala is a presenter of news and factual programming for the BBC, appearing most notably on *Crimewatch* and *News 24*.

He was born in Leeds in 1962, and, after graduating from Durham University with a degree in Law and Politics, worked as an accountant before joining the BBC.

His rather unusual name was originally even more unusual: Mehrwan F. Amroliwalla.

BADBOY MATTHEWS

Robert Matthews was a self-styled religious prophet who flourished in America in the 1830s. At various times, he called himself Matthias the Prophet, or The Spirit of Truth.

Matthews' beliefs were bizarre and distinctive. Although superficially a variant of Christianity, deep down he harboured a profound hatred for Christianity, blaming it for "feminising" the human population and weakening the bonds of male patriarchy over the course of 1800 years.

Matthews was the ultimate male chauvinist. He believed women should be utterly submissive to the male, and should be denied any form of education. He also believed that the spirit of a man was literally passed down through the ages from father to son, in a kind of quasi-reincarnation. On this basis, for example, he claimed both to be, and to be the descendant of, Saint Matthias, the 13th Apostle, who had replaced Judas Iscariot.

As in more modern cults, Matthews' prophet antics tended to involve as much the appropriation of his followers' labour, money and wives as they did religion. The whole thing collapsed amid scandal and criminal charges following the death of one of his followers. Matthews was charged with murder but acquitted.

He was also charged with blasphemy but the charge was dropped when, awkwardly, the prosecution found itself unable to prove that he was not the messiah.

Curiously, 150 years after self-styled prophet Robert Matthews founded a cult in New York, another Robert Mathews founded another cult-like group in America too, this time in the Pacific North-west region.

The modern **Robert Jay Mathews** was a neo-nazi who founded a group called The Order, also known as Bruders Schweigen (Silent Brotherhood), a name he borrowed from the Nazi SS. Over several years, the gang committed a series of robberies in order to raise funds. One of these was spectacularly successful, netting more than $3 million.

In the end, though, it was this operation which was to lead to Mathews' downfall, because he inadvertently left a pistol at the scene which the police were able to trace to a member of his group.

In 1984, members of The Order murdered controversial left-wing talk-show host, Alan Berg, outside his home in Denver, Colorado. Berg had provoked the ire of the group by mocking racists and right-wingers who called in to the show. Two members of The Order were ultimately sentenced to life imprisonment for the Berg killing.

Robert Mathews was not among them. By the time the trial came around, he was already dead, killed in a shoot-out with the FBI after they finally tracked him down. Impressively, he managed to hold off a 200-man siege force for 36 hours before meeting his demise; unimpressively, he chose to barricade himself in with boxes of ammunition, a decision which played a significant role in bringing said demise about, after a magnesium flare set off a chain detonation.

Matthew Gregory Lewis was a British writer and
Member of Parliament who, thanks to his racy gothic novel
The Monk, which he penned at the age of 19, for a time
enjoyed a reputation as a kind of British Marquis de Sade.
Even the "Bad Lord Byron" hailed him as follows:

Oh! wonder-working Lewis! monk, or bard!
Who fain wouldst make Parnassus a churchyard!
…Whether on ancient tombs thou tak'st thy stand,
By gibb'ring spectres hail'd, thy kindred band!
…All hail, M.P.! from whose infernal brain
Thin-sheeted phantoms glide, a grisly train.
…Even Satan's self with thee might dread to dwell,
And in thy skull discern a deeper hell.

In less piquant verse, which he placed in the preface to his
own book, Lewis described himself as:

Of passions strong, of hasty nature,
Of graceless form and dwarfish stature;
By few approved, and few approving;
Extreme in hating and in loving.

Lewis had made a study of foreign languages to prepare
himself for a career in the diplomatic service. All of his
work shows the influence of the German gothic tradition, in
particular, and he later published a number of translations
from German.

Despite his badboy reputation, Lewis showed a signal
concern for the well-being of those who worked on his
far-flung plantations. A visit to his plantations in the West

Indies inspired him to write *The Journal of a West Indian Proprietor*, which was not published until after his death. On a trip to Jamaica in 1817, Lewis contracted a fever which led to his death, aged 42, while on the ship home.

You've heard of an employee buy-out? Well, **Matthew Beck** went one better and had an employee shoot-out.

In 1998, Beck was a 35-year-old accountant working for the state lottery commission in Connecticut. Disgruntled with his pay and promotion prospects, he took a leave of absence to recover from stress. Apparently, it didn't work though, because when he came back he decided to go on a killing spree through the company offices, targeting the top executives, managing to bag four in total. When police confronted him, he shot and killed himself.

Mathew Bevan was the classic nerd who was bullied at school and found happiness in the world of his computer. Born in Cardiff, he managed to achieve the distinction of being called "the greatest threat to world peace since Adolf Hitler" by a Pentagon spokesman. Bevan, an *X-Files* fan steeped in UFO conspiracy theories, was intent on using his computer skills to find evidence that the US government had secret relations with aliens, and was in possession of alien technology. To this end, he hacked into a variety of top secret military installations around the world, including a nuclear research facility in Korea.

In 1999, Bevan was charged with Intent to Secure Unauthorised Access to Computer Systems. Online, Bevan had used the handle Kuji and when his case was discussed in the US Senate, it was made to seem that he was some dastardly foreign spy, perhaps Chinese in origin.

Publicity about his hacking adventures brought some undesirable consequences. He began to receive bizarre, threatening phone calls, many of which seemed to come from Asians. To escape these, he was forced to move house. Fearing for his life, he decided to go public with more details of what he had done, thinking that, if it was all in the public domain, there would be no further reason to kill him.

In his online forays, Bevan claimed he had come across documents relating to an anti-gravity propulsion system, capable of achieving speeds of up to Mach 18. The case played out over a number of years but, eventually, the Crown Prosecution Service decided that there was no further public interest in pursuing it.

How would you choose to spend your last moments before execution?

Charles Guiteau (1841-1882) chose to spend them reciting 14 verses from the Gospel of Matthew followed by a self-penned poem with the immortal first line "I am going to the Lordy, I am so glad".

He had requested an orchestra to accompany him but the authorities declined to honour his request.

Of all the lone nuts who have assassinated America's presidents over the years, Guiteau was undoubtedly the nuttiest. Aggrieved at not being offered a diplomatic position he believed he was entitled to, Guiteau determined to seek revenge by shooting President James Garfield in July 1881. Garfield lived for 81 days after the shooting, allowing Guiteau to defend himself by arguing that he was not responsible for the President's death; his incompetent doctors were.

While awaiting trial, Guiteau penned a bizarre autobiography, and advertised for a wife. He behaved strangely throughout the trial, sometimes sending notes to members of the audience, asking their advice about how he should proceed, for example.

After conviction, Guiteau's final hope rested with President Arthur, newly elevated from the Vice Presidency. Guiteau wrote Arthur a letter, telling him he owed him for the promotion. Arthur declined to grant clemency and Guiteau was duly executed.

Crop circle mania seized Britain in the 1980s and early 1990s. Were the mysterious symbols imprinted in the fields signs from aliens, as some believed?

A result of a hitherto little-understood weather phenomenon?

No, they were the result of two old guys, Doug and Dave, having a bit of a laugh with a plank after they'd been down the pub.

The Doug and Dave confession deflated the crop circle movement greatly, but did not kill it off. Diehards claimed that, while some of the circles had undoubtedly been faked, others were real. Doug and Dave, they hinted, might even have been working for MI5, going public with a fake confession to throw investigators off the alien trail.

Those who thought the whole thing was a fake were derisively dubbed "plankers" by the true believers. **Matthew Williams** was the king of the plankers. While the believers insisted that the patterns found in the fields (which had evolved into something far more elaborate than the simple circles) were mystic communications from Beyond and could not possibly have been produced by plank-wielding idiots in the dark, Matthew was determined to prove them wrong.

So successful was he in this goal that he became the first ever crop circle-maker to be prosecuted for his "art" after the police obtained photographs of him engaged in corn-gouging. A court fined him £100 for criminal damage. Not deterred, he later released a three-hour video detailing the activities of his fellow "corn sculptors".

Matthew Hardman, a 17-year-old from North Wales, was dubbed the "Vampire Killer" after murdering his 90-year old neighbour in 2001. It was not that Hardman wanted to slay vampires.

He wanted to become one. In fact, a few weeks before committing the murder, he had asked a German girl to bite him in the neck, because he believed she was a vampire and he, too, wanted to become "one of them". Not surprisingly, she called for help.

His desire to become immortal remained, however, and, a few weeks later, it was his neighbour, Mabel Leyshon, who fell victim to it. Hardman broke into her home while she was watching television and stabbed her 22 times.

Afterwards, he mutilated her body, removed her heart and placed it in a saucepan. He drained her blood into the saucepan and drank it, placing two pokers at her feet in the shape of a cross.

It was only after interviewing every male in the neighbourhood that the police began to suspect Hardman. His answers appeared inconsistent, and they proceeded to do DNA testing. When a match was found, he was arrested and charged.

Psychologists who examined Hardman during the trial could find no trace of mental illness. To all outward appearances, he seemed to be a polite and normal boy. The judge speculated that he suffered from a "disguised mental illness" and sentenced him to a minimum of 12 years imprisonment.

"But every military leader, from the lowest to the highest, owes it to the men whose lives are at his disposal to speak out clearly when he feels that a serious mistake is about to be made"

GEN Matthew Ridgway

STORMY MATTHEW

The US National Weather Service first adopted the practice of naming hurricanes in 1953. At first, only female names were used, allotted in alphabetical order from a list prepared at the beginning of each year. Men's names were added in 1979 in a gesture to gender equality.

The practice has since spread internationally and has been formalised through the World Meteorological Association. Normally, a list of locally-appropriate names is submitted by each region where tropical storms occur. Those names are then selected randomly as the storms manifest themselves. When a particularly egregious storm breaks out, its name is withdrawn from the list forever, so it will be remembered as a unique event.

Matthew is in the naming list for tropical storms in the North Atlantic region. So far, its sole brush with infamy came in 2004 when **Tropical Storm Matthew** emerged in Africa and swept across the Atlantic to hit land in the south-eastern United States.

Alas, Matthew utterly failed to cut it as a bad boy. He caused no deaths and only about $200-300,000 worth of damage. In fact, using the wind speed-based classification system, Matthew barely rated as a tropical storm at all (39-73 mph) and came nowhere near qualifying to become a hurricane (74 mph).

Because Matthew wasn't powerful enough to earn himself eternal fame, the name has been recycled back into the pool, giving him another chance at the big time some time in the future.

Somewhere, sometime, there will be a devastating hurricane called Matthew which will wreak havoc on some unfortunate part of the world, its name seared forever into the shattered psyches of the survivors and embedded eternally in the folk memory of the region.

It's just a question of time.

———◇———

"I never set out to be rich and famous. I wanted to follow my own path"
Matthew Modine

WHEN WILL MATTHEW BE FAMOUS?

Along with his twin brother Luke, **Matt Goss** formed the core of the short-lived 1980s boy band Bros.

They had no talent whatsoever but, despite that, managed to score a few hit singles on the strength of their good looks. Over the course of a five-year career, the band achieved 11 Top 40 singles in total, and three respectably-selling albums, before breaking up in 1992.

Afterwards, Matt embarked on a solo music career, but he has so far been unable to recreate his earlier commercial success.

MORE MATTHEW BADBOYS

Mary Shelley's *Frankenstein* tells the story of the mad scientist who tries to resuscitate the dead. At the time, it was far from the wild flight of fancy it now appears today, however. Real experiments of that very nature were occurring all over Europe. One of the most notable took place in Glasgow in 1818, the very same year that *Frankenstein* was published.

The unhappy experimental subject was **Matthew Clydesdale**, a muscular man of around 30 who had just been hanged for murdering his 70-year-old neighbour. Dr. Andrew Ure, professor of chemistry and natural philosophy at Anderson College in Glasgow, led the experiment.

He applied electrical stimulation to various parts of the unfortunate Clydesdale's body, and observed the effects. When the diaphragm and left phrenic nerve were stimulated, the result, Ure said, was "truly wonderful".

The corpse recommenced breathing. The chest heaved and fell, the lungs inhaled and exhaled, in the simple rhythm of life. By applying stimulation in another place, Ure was able to elicit a wide range of facial expressions, seemingly embodying everything from amusement to rage. So lifelike was the display that some members of the audience fainted.

Ure was worried that, if he had succeeded in reviving his subject, he might have been breaking the law, since Clydesdale, after all, had been condemned to death by a court of law.

Some accounts claim that Ure was forced to cut the jugular of Matthew Clydesdale's corpse after it showed too many signs of being re-animated, but this is almost certainly an apocryphal detail slipped into later accounts to embellish the tale.

One of the most notorious Australian bush-rangers was called **Matthew Brady** (1799-1826). Born in Manchester, after a brief career in the military Brady was shipped out to the Australian penal colonies for a minor crime.

After protesting at the conditions in which he was kept, he was dispatched to the even harsher Sarah Colony in Van Diemen's Land, an island off the main Australian continent now known as Tasmania.

Matthew didn't much care for the conditions there either. Fortunately, he didn't have to endure them for long, successfully making his escape into the surrounding wilderness. There he formed a gang of criminal desperadoes who raided settlements and robbed travellers.

In the course of these criminal ventures, Brady became known for his courtesy in dealing with his victims, particularly women.

After a shoot-out at the town of Launceston, legendary bounty hunter John Batman (who would later found the city of Melbourne) captured Brady and collected the reward. Matthew Brady was hanged on the morning of May 4th 1826, the cell which he had quit for the last time reportedly filled with flowers sent by the local women who wept bitterly at his passing.

(He has been called Australia's first sex symbol.)

In June 2008 **Matthew Whitton** claimed to have discovered what had eluded scientific researchers, cryptozoologists, and amateur investigators of the weird for decades: proof of bigfoot – the fabled half-man, half-ape.

Stories of the mysterious creature had circulated in North America for generations, but no proof had ever been found. Along with his friend Rick Dyer, Whitton claimed that he had come across a dead bigfoot while on an expedition in Georgia. Allegedly worried that the body of the unfortunate creature would rot before they were able to show it to the world, they decided to encase it in ice.

Announcing their find to the press and on YouTube, they proclaimed it "the greatest find of the millennium". The announcement provoked a stir worldwide, with masses of media coverage.

The pair had promised to present the dead creature to the public, along with "DNA evidence" on a specified date. When the date arrived, though, they had scarpered. The ice had been melted to reveal nothing more than a cheap gorilla costume.

Amazingly, both men were involved in law enforcement. Whitton was a police officer, on medical leave after having inadvertently shot himself while chasing a bank robber.

Dyer was a prison officer. After the hoax was revealed, Whitton was immediately sacked.

Not deterred, before long the two men were boasting about the hoax on their website, promising to release a DVD called *Bigfoot Doesn't Live*.

Matthew Quintal was one of the famous mutineers who took over *The Bounty*. Most modern portrayals of the story represent the ship's captain, Bligh, as a tyrant and the mutineers as decent blokes who just wanted a bit of a cuddle with the native women.

The reality seems to have been somewhat different. Matthew, in particular, was a world-class bad boy. Indeed, he was the first one Bligh felt it necessary to flog, for "insolence and insubordination", thus setting the whole chain of events in motion. He was also the one to whom Fletcher Christian first proposed the mutiny.

In 1790, Quintal was one of the nine mutineers who, along with six native men and eleven native women, settled on a small island now known as Pitcairn Island. They worked out how to distil alcohol from the local ti plants and were thus able to get wildly drunk at will.

With such a small group, the swapping of sexual partners provoked rivalries and tensions. This culminated in violence between the native men and the British mutineers. All of the native men perished, as did five of the British, including the ringleader, Fletcher Christian.

Matthew Quintal survived the initial carnage but not for long. His violent temper made the others on the island afraid of him, particularly when he was intoxicated. After he demanded possession of Fletcher Christian's widow, Isabella, threatening violence if he was denied, the others decided he had to be done away with. He was lured into one of the islander's homes and murdered with an axe.

Pitcairn Island is still inhabited today, and is a UK Overseas Territory.

⟫◆⟪

"I had a philosophy, which may have been proven right, that directing isn't as hard as everyone says it is"
Matthew Vaughn

POET MATTHEWS

Matthew Prior was an English poet and diplomat of the late 17th and early 18th centuries. Born the son of a joiner in 1664, his father died while he was still young and he was raised by his uncle, who put him to work in his tavern.

The Earl of Dorset, a frequent visitor to the establishment, one day stumbled on Prior reading Horace, and impressed by his ability to produce an extempore English translation of the Latin poet, decided to pay for his further education.

After graduating from Cambridge, Matthew was appointed to a diplomatic position. In the years to come he would participate in much of the diplomacy occasioned by the wars of Louis XIV.

Indeed, Prior played a key role in the secret negotiations which preceded the signing of the Treaty of Utrecht, which finally brought the War of the Spanish Succession to an end. The out-of-favour Whig party was adamantly opposed to the treaty and derisively dubbed it "Matt's Peace".

Prior called himself a "poet by accident" whose work was mostly written in the idle moments of his public career. Although his subject matter was usually derivative, his versification was acknowledged to be of a very high standard.

Prior died in 1721 and is buried at Poets' Corner in Westminster Abbey.

Matthew Arnold (1822-1888) was one of the last great English poets before the onset of modernism.

Arnold was appointed to the Oxford chair of poetry in 1857, and, in his later years, literary and cultural criticism dominated his output, most of his poetry being written by the time he had reached his mid 40s. He retained an affection for Oxford throughout his life, and it was he who coined the phrase the "dreaming spires" of Oxford in his poem *Thyrsis*.

As in the example below, much of his poetry has a solemn, valedictory tone, as if he sensed that the grand classical world he knew and loved was ebbing away, to be replaced by something more modern, vigorous and uncouth.

The Sea of Faith
Was once, too, at the full, and round earth's shore
Lay like the folds of a bright girdle furl'd.
But now I only hear
Its melancholy, long, withdrawing roar,
Retreating, to the breath
Of the night-wind, down the vast edges drear
And naked shingles of the world.

Arnold's subjects were often drawn from Olde World tales and mythology, and he wrote several poems about people who shrugged off the modern world and lived an eremitic existence dedicated to art.

Matthew Green was a minor poet of the early 18th century. His best-known work is a longish single poem called *Spleen*, written in Hudibrastic couplets, in which he advises a friend on how to avoid the perils of deep depression. His verse is fresh and unpretentious in style, containing the odd remarkable passage here and there.

Spleen was praised by both Alexander Pope and Thomas Gray, and earned Matthew the nickname of Spleen Green. Some people even believe he was a one hit wonder who wrote no other poems. This is not true, but *Spleen* was certainly his high point.

Happy the man who, innocent,
Grieves not at ills he can't prevent;
His skiff does with the current glide,
Not puffing pulled against the tide.
He, paddling by the scuffling crowd,
Sees unconcerned life's wager row'd,
And when he can't prevent foul play,
Enjoys the folly of the fray.

Matthew Green was raised by strict Quaker parents but later rebelled against his upbringing and discarded the Quaker faith. He earned his living in a customs house, and died unmarried and childless at the age of only 41.

The great poet William Wordsworth wrote a number of poems about a mysterious figure called "**Matthew**", seemingly a rustic sage and a source of inspiration to everyone he encountered.

A schoolmaster by title known
Long Matthew penned his little flock
Within yon pile that stands alone
In colour like its native rock.

Learning will often dry the heart,
The very bones it will distress,
But Matthew had an idle art
Of teaching love and happiness.

Some of the poems are so heartfelt that you would swear
this Matthew must have been an intimate acquaintance and
a shaping influence on Wordsworth's life.

Actually, though, he was a complete fiction. No real
Matthew existed. But scholars believe the character
was a kind of composite figure based on several people
Wordsworth had encountered, and been inspired by, in
real life, including the schoolmaster William Taylor and an
unnamed wandering salesman whose homespun philosophy
is said to have impressed the poet deeply during his
adolescent years.

A MATTHEW READ BY BILLIONS

Whenever you are flipping through your favourite magazine or newspaper, or reading something online, there's a good chance you'll be encountering the work of a Matthew who has touched the lives of perhaps more than any other, but, except to the cognoscenti, is almost completely unknown: **Matthew Carter**, typeface designer.

Matthew acquired an interested in typefaces from his typographer father, and studied the old craft methods in the Netherlands before embarking on a successful international career as a type designer.

He has designed typefaces for high-profile publications such as *Time* and *Newsweek* magazines, the *Washington Post* and the American phone book. When the digital revolution arrived, Matthew moved with the times, designing what became the quintessential web font, Verdana, for Microsoft.

CREATIVE MATTHEWS

Matthew Fisher was a founder member of Procol Harum – which roughly means 'beyond these things' in Latin – who formed in April 1967. He was to contribute the most distinctive element of the band's sound – its pseudo-classical Hammond organ lines.

In 1967 the band recorded its masterpiece: Whiter Shade of Pale, a song with surrealist (some say meaningless, although debate continues to rage) lyrics and an organ part which was a homage to Bach.

Within 2 weeks, it had reached number one in Britain and remained there for six weeks. It sold similarly well overseas.

Matthew Fisher remained a member of the band until 1969. He rejoined in 1991, only to quit finally in 2004. Over all those years of his membership in the band, a dispute had been simmering. It related to who the authors of Whiter Shade of Pale were. Gary Brooker, the band's founder, claimed that he was the sole author. It had been suggested, however, that Fisher, as creator of the organ part, should have been given a co-author credit and a share of the royalties.

When Fisher raised the issue after leaving the band, he got nowhere. Legal action ensued. The initial 2006 verdict was favourable: It was decided that Fisher's part in the song was indeed so distinctive that he should be credited as its co-author and given a 40% share of its royalties, a sum which might have amounted to more than one million pounds.

Two years later, however, this judgement was modified on appeal. Fisher's claim to co-authorship was upheld but he was denied any royalties on the grounds that he had waited too long before asserting his rights. Mystified by the verdict, Fisher claimed he was content because he had at last won credit for his contribution and wasn't that bothered about the million quid.

Yeah right, Matthew. We believe you.

Matthew Locke was a British baroque composer who was born in Devon in 1622. He learned music as a chorister at Exeter Cathedral and would compose a number of notable choral works in the course of his career. As well as religiously-inspired pieces, he composed music for secular drama, including the works of William Davenant. One fruit of this collaboration, in 1656, was The Siege of Rhodes, which some have called the first English opera.

Locke also composed music for the royal court, including a piece for the coronation of Charles II in 1661. This led to his appointment as Composer in Ordinary.
Henry Purcell, ultimately a greater composer than Locke, composed a moving elegy to him and is believed to have been one of his pupils. He died in London in 1677.

Matt Cutts is one of Google's principal software engineers. Among other things, he has been responsible for making Google searches family-friendly and became famous within the company for giving his wife's home-made biscuits to anyone who could show him an unwanted porn link in a set of search results.

Thanks to his public appearances and his blog, he has become one of Google's best known public faces. He has also attracted negative attention from conspiracy theorists who make much of his student placement with America's National Security Agency (NSA), which spies on communications around the world.

According to anti-Google campaigners, the company is in bed with the CIA, and is harvesting reams of data on people all over the world to hand over on demand to the spooks at Langley.

Rodney Matthews (b. 1945) is a British fantasy artist whose work has appeared on millions of posters and album covers worldwide. He has enjoyed a long association with sword and sorcery supremo Michael Moorcock, penning the cover art for many of his books. Most of Matthews' album covers have been done for heavy metal acts, including such big names as Thin Lizzy, Asia and Nazareth.

The mid 17th century was a time of mad passion in England, as Civil War tensions gathered, raged and abated. Few were able to remain level-headed in the midst of such turmoil. One of those few was **Sir Matthew Hale** (1609-1676). Though raised as a Puritan, as a barrister he vigorously defended Royalists who came before the courts.

When later appointed a judge by Oliver Cromwell in 1654, he acquired a reputation for even-handedness. Indeed, tempering the harshness of the law with the wisdom of common sense and basic decency was to be characteristic of Matthew throughout his life. One notable exception, however, was when he allowed two unfortunate women to be convicted of witchcraft and subsequently hanged.

Matthew was known for his indefatigable reading habits. When considering a point of law, he would read literally everything that had ever been written on the subject. As a consequence, the judgements he made were often spot on, and the summaries he gave of specific points of law became the bedrock of the growing corpus of English legal knowledge.

His relentlessly curious mind did not confine itself to the law, however; he read voraciously in other fields, acquiring the kind of well-furnished intellect which added depth and nuance to the quality of his legal opinions.

Matthew also served as a Member of Parliament and played a key part in advocating for the restoration of Charles II.

Matt Mullenweg (b. 1984) gave voice to the masses by creating the Wordpress blogging platform. No longer would people be forced to recount the dull experiences of their humdrum lives, and commit pointless, half-baked thoughts and opinions to perishable paper diaries which no one would ever read.

Now, via the internet, pointless, half-baked thoughts and opinions are broadcast for all the world to see. Too many trees died to record what wasn't worth recording. Now electrons only shuffle around a bit. That's what I call progress.

Matthew Rolston (b. 1955) is one of the most admired celebrity photographers in the world. His work has appeared in numerous glossy magazines and has been hugely influential, defining a style which combines modernity with classical elegance.

Matthew grew up in Hollywood, where his grandfather worked as a dentist to the stars. His early ideas of beauty were shaped by the signed photographs of stars and starlets from Hollywood's golden age which adorned the waiting-room walls at his grandfather's dental practice.

You've probably heard of J. M. Barrie (1860-1937), author of *Peter Pan*. But did you know he was a secret Matthew? That's right. The "M" in his name stands for Matthew, and his full name is **James Matthew Barrie**.

Born in Kirriemuir in Scotland, and educated at the University of Edinburgh, Barrie soon carved out a career for himself as a writer. His early works were mostly sentimental novels of no real literary distinction, but they proved popular with the public and earned him a good living.

He first wrote *Peter Pan* as a play, subtitled *The Boy Who Wouldn't Grow Up*, and later novelised by Barrie himself as *Peter and Wendy*. It was, at least in part, autobiographical, insofar as Barrie was something of a child-man himself. At only five feet tall, he had the stature of an adolescent.

He also appeared to be devoid of any sexual feeling. Although he married actress Mary Ansell in 1894, they had no children and the marriage may well never have been consummated. The couple divorced in 1909.

Despite his childlike nature, Barrie was no recluse. He moved in high social circles, mingling freely with the great and good. His circle of acquaintances included George Bernard Shaw and Robert Louis Stevenson; he even read stories to the future Queen Elizabeth II and Princess Margaret when the two were still children.

Barrie vested the copyright of the work with Great Ormond Street children's hospital in London.

Matt Stone (b. 1971) was one of the creators of the phenomenally-successful animated series *South Park*.

South Park followed where *The Simpsons* had blazed a trail, showing that wit and originality could prove an acceptable substitute for high-grade production values.

Based around a group of schoolchildren in a small, fictional Colorado town, *South Park* mercilessly lampoons everything from celebs to religions. In fact, the satire went a bit too far for one of the cast members when the show took on Scientology.

Isaac Hayes, a former 1970s soul artist who voiced the character Chef, was himself a scientologist and felt impelled to resign shortly thereafter.

Matt Stone and Trey Parker, the co-creator, originally met at the University of Colorado where each was taking a film class. Later, they made a short film called *The Spirit of Christmas* which featured Jesus and Santa fighting each other over the spirit of Christmas, and, after it was circulated by some Hollywood friends, led to them being offered a show on the Comedy Channel.

The resultant *South Park* was an immediate success and some say it single-handedly rescued The Comedy Channel from failure.

Matthew Bellamy is the lead singer, song-writer, guitarist and general creative force behind the group Muse. He is the son of George Bellamy, member of the band The Tornados, which had a global hit in the 60s with Telstar. The band's music is difficult to pigeonhole, resembling heavy metal in parts but often breaking with the genre conventions by incorporating mellow passages and synthesizer elements. "Alternative rock" is the label usually applied.

Bellamy has been hailed as one of the greatest guitarists of all time, regularly placing within the top 50 when polls are taken in guitar magazines. His guitars are custom-made by

Hugh Manson and are known as "Mattocasters" because they are based on the Fender Telecaster. He also has a reputation as a heartthrob, being named "Sexiest Male" by NME in 2007.

"They never taste who always drink: They always talk, who never think"
Matthew Prior

MORE CREATIVE MATTHEWS

Dave Matthews (b. 1967) is a musician whose eponymous band has managed to achieve the rare combination of chart success and critical credibility. Mixing jazz elements with a rock sound, the Dave Matthews Band injects a special creativity into its live performances, which feature long sequences of passionate improvisation.

This has led to comparisons with the hippy favourites, the Grateful Dead. Like the famous deadheads, the Dave Matthews Band fans eagerly trade recordings of notable live gigs, both bootlegs and official releases.

Matthew Noble (1818-1876) was a British sculptor whose work adorned many British cities in the Victorian age. Among his more notable pieces are:

The figure of Albert at the Albert Memorial in Manchester.

Figures of Robert Peel at Parliament Square in London and in St. George's Hall in Liverpool.

Matt Harding (b. 1976) was a humble computer programmer who got tired of the rat race and decided to do a bit of travelling for a while. While in Vietnam, he impulsively made a video of himself dancing in Hanoi and uploaded it to YouTube. It proved a huge hit so he kept on doing it…

Matt has produced many videos of himself doing his rather uncomplicated dance moves in notable places all around the world, sometimes on his own and sometimes joined by swarms of enthusiastic locals. His efforts can be seen on his website at: www.wherethehellismatt.com

The **St. Matthew Passion** is often considered the finest work of the great German composer Johann Sebastian Bach. Although Bach himself was a strict Lutheran, his work is admired by Protestants and Catholics alike.

Matt Drudge (b. 1966) was the first of a new generation of internet journalists to make it big. Always a keen reader of news, but hampered by his lack of educational credentials, Drudge could only get a job in the gift shop at CBS. His journalistic instincts found life on the web, however, where he could get away with peddling rumour to a much greater extent than was possible in the print media.

Drudge broke the story that not only had Bill Clinton had an affair with a 23-year-old intern, but the popular news magazine *Newsweek* had decided not to run a story about it. The scandal snowballed and soon Clinton found himself facing impeachment.

Although technically not a blogger himself, Drudge was the first to demonstrate the subversive power of the internet in taking on the journalistic establishment.

Ironically, considering the fact that he had published a number of pieces claiming that prominent politicians were closet homosexuals, Drudge himself was later rumoured to be gay. He rarely does interviews and has shown an obsessive concern with his own privacy.

The Drudge Report website is still regarded as one of the world's top ten. Journalists flock to it to find tips, and everything from Hollywood studios to presidential campaigns use it to feed their news titbits to the world. Its popularity has made Drudge a multi-millionaire, and he now owns several homes in Florida and California.

PIONEERING MATTHEW

Matthew Smith (b. 1966) was the teenage bedroom programmer who created two of the earliest computer games in Britain: Manic Miner and Jet Set Willy. They are still remembered affectionately by an entire generation of British males, for whom the ZX Spectrum was the PlayStation of the day.

A third game in the series, titled Manic Miner Meets the Taxman in a wry reference to the difficulties Matthew's newfound wealth had brought him, was rumoured but never appeared.

Like the French poet Rimbaud, who wrote some of the best French poetry ever at the age of 15-16, then decided to give up the writing of poetry forever and go off to Africa to become an arms dealer for the rest of his life, at the peak of his success Matthew Smith decided to walk away from it all.

He never wrote another game and disappeared from public view entirely. Glimpses of him were reported like sightings of Elvis.

A website (www.whereismatthewsmith.com) was even set up to collate sighting reports. It was said he had settled in Amsterdam and joined a commune. This turned out to be true, as Matthew confirmed when he eventually re-surfaced and did a television interview.

Discussing his famous disappearing act, he joked, "Five years later I was a wash-out. Ten years later I was history. Twenty years later, I'm a legend."

MATTHEW, CREATOR OF A GLOBAL PHENOMENON

Matt Groening is the man behind *The Simpsons*, the hippy cartoonist who built a billion-dollar business empire despite the lack of any obvious ability to draw.

After studying at Evergreen State College in Olympia, Washington, which was popular with free-minded flower power types thanks to its complete absence of any curriculum or attendance requirements, Groening began work in a series of low-end jobs around the country, eventually graduating to a low-end job in L.A.

His first venture into cartoon satire was the comic strip *Life in Hell*, which started life as a kind of substitute letter home to his family to let them know how things were going in the city of aspiring waiters.

It was an instant hit, being passed around among friends and acquaintances. Soon it was being distributed in the record shop where Groening worked behind the counter.

There, too, it proved popular. Eventually, it was picked up by a number of alternative weeklies in the city and developed a cult following. When Fox Television was looking for a filler for the Tracey Ullman comedy show, they gave Groening a call.

Although they originally wanted him to use the characters from *Life in Hell*, he preferred to develop new ones, naming them after the members of his own family.

As *The Simpsons*, the filler proved more popular than the show itself and was soon rewarded with a slot of its own. Its quietly subversive humour was a worldwide hit, and earned a fortune both for Fox, and Groening.

CONSERVATIVE MATTHEW

Matthew Parris is a political commentator and
parliamentary sketch writer who once served a stint as a
Conservative MP under Margaret Thatcher.

Openly homosexual, he has been called one of Britain's
most influential gay men, and famously once outed
Labour's Peter Mandelson in the course of a *Newsnight*
broadcast.

Parris was born in South Africa and had a varied,
cosmopolitan upbringing as he followed in the footsteps of
his globe-trotting father. This relish for foreign travel and
adventure remained with him into his adult years.

Parris participated in a number of "extreme" travel
expeditions, including climbs of Mount Kilimanjaro, and
once clocked up a highly respectable time of 2 hours 32
minutes while running the London marathon.

MATTHEW SMITHS

Matthew Smith
– 18th century Vice-President (Lt. Gov.) of Pennsylvania

Matthew Smith
– British parapsychologist

Matthew Smith (1836-1887)
– former acting Colonial Secretary of Western Australia

Matthew Smith (1879-1959)
– British painter

Matthew H. Smith (b. 1972)
– Pennsylvania politician

Matthew Smith (b. 1973)
– Australian field hockey player

Matthew Dow Smith
– American comic book artist

UNREAL MATTHEWS

Matt Murdock is the real name of the Marvel Comics superhero Daredevil. Raised in a tough New York neighbourhood, Matt's life was changed forever when he saved a blind man from being run over by a truck carrying radioactive material.

Unfortunately, some of the material spilled out, rendering Matt blind for life himself. Although he could no longer see, he found that his other senses had become super-sensitive. When Matt's father, a boxer, was murdered by a villain for refusing to take a dive in a fight, Matthew Murdock decided to take on the criminals: as Daredevil.

Daredevil has been one of Marvel's most popular superheroes for decades, starting in the 1960s and continuing until the present day. The hero reached a wider public through the release of the 2003 Hollywood film, *Daredevil*, featuring Ben Affleck in the lead role.

Matt Monro was a celebrated British crooner who went from bus driver to international star singing syrupy ballads. His real name was Terence Edward Parsons. In the 1950s he struggled to earn a living but hit the big time in the 1960s.

The world of cinema proved to be his passport to greater things. Throughout his career, Matt Monro always had a special relationship with cinema, recording keynote songs for films like *Born Free* (for which he became best known),

The Italian Job, and the James Bond films *From Russia With Love* and *Thunderball*. Among his other notable hits were *Portrait of My Love* and *Walk Away*, an English-language version of a song originally written in German, *Warum Nur Warum*, which Monro first heard while competing in the 1964 Eurovision song contest (he came second).

Matt Monro died in London in 1985 at the age of only 55. His son, Matthew (b. 1964), also became a singer and, using the stage name Matt Monro Jr., gave tribute band-style public performances of his father's music, even releasing a pseudo duet album in which his own voice was mixed in with a recording of his father's.

Matthew Corbett (b. 1948) is a performer and television personality best known to a generation of British children for having his hand stuck up the rear end of a bear, specifically Sooty the Bear. Sooty was a yellow sock puppet which Matthew's father, Harry, bought from a magic shop in Blackpool and then made nationally famous on television.

Sooty was essentially a ventriloquist act without the "gottle of gear" ventriloquism. Harry made life easy on himself with the conceit that Sooty could only speak in whispers so he would have to lean in very close to hear what he was saying.

When Harry retired in 1976, Matthew, who was already working in children's television with the Rod, Matt and Jane musical trio, took the show over. Matthew's real name is Peter but, because there was already another performer named Peter Corbett, he adopted the name Matthew for all of his entertainment work.

In Matthew's capable hand, *The Sooty Show* remained a fixture on British children's television until he retired in 1998. Recently, another performer has bought the rights to Sooty and hopes to revive its popularity with a younger generation.

Since retiring from *The Sooty Show*, Matthew has performed as a rock'n'roll singer in pub gigs around Manchester under his real name.

Matthew Star was the eponymous hero of an American television series named *The Powers of Matthew Star*. Debuting in 1982, it starred Peter Barton as the protagonist, seemingly an ordinary teenage boy who, in reality, was a prince from a planet called Quadris.

Forced to quit his homeworld after it was conquered by evil alien invaders, Matthew fled to Earth to plot his revenge. Like all members of his family, Matthew had an assortment of extraordinary mental abilities, including telekinesis and telepathy. He developed these powers on Earth while attending school and doing his homework like every other teenager.

Many of the episodes involved Matthew and his faithful sidekick Walt, played by Louis Gossett Jr., fending off attacks from alien agents sent to assassinate them. A suspicious FBI agent also investigates the pair.

Alas, *The Powers of Matthew Star* failed to click with audiences and was shown for only one season.

The Disney animated series *Gargoyles*, which ran from 1994 to 1997, was aimed at a more mature audience than most cartoons and was notable for featuring the voice talents of a number of ex-Star Trek actors.

Its storyline featured six stone gargoyles who had been transported from medieval Scotland to the summit of a skyscraper in New York, from where they would fend off threats to the city from various hostile forces. **Matt Bluestone** was one of the key characters in the series, voiced by Thomas F. Wilson.

Bluestone was a young police officer obsessed with proving the existence of a mysterious secret society known as the Illuminati; later on, he becomes aware of the gargoyles and learns of the Illuminati's great interest in them.

It emerges that his partner, Elisa, has known of the gargoyles' existence for some time and had become their protector, trying to keep them safe from prying eyes. Matt Bluestone eventually becomes complicit in this arrangement.

The series ran for only two seasons but developed a cult following. A comic now continues where the television series left off.

Matthew of Westminster was a medieval chronicler who didn't even exist. For a long time he was wrongly believed to have been the author of *Flores Historiarum* (The Flowers of History), which we now know was written by the more famous medieval chronicler Matthew Paris. The error was first discovered in 1826 by Francis Turner Palgrave.

It seems Matthew Paris may have authored his works in more than one place, giving rise to the initial confusion, which persisted for centuries – with many books talking about Matthew of Westminster as if he was a real person – before being cleared up in more modern times.

DULL AS MATTHEW

Matti Vanhanen has been the Prime Minister of Finland since 2003.

He is generally considered staggeringly boring by almost everyone, a kind of Finnish John Major.

The only real spice in his political career came when a woman he had met through an internet dating service (while Prime Minister) broke off the relationship and wrote a tell-all book about it. The resultant publicity actually ended up boosting his popularity.

⟾◆⟾

"Eventually stardom is going to go away from me. It goes away from everybody and all you have in the end is to be able to look back and like the choices you made"
Matt Damon

Play it again, Matthew

Matt Aitken (b. 1956) was one of the infamous trio of Stock, Aitken and Waterman (SAW) who dominated British pop in the 1980s. They achieved something like an industrial mass production system for pop music in which they would write and record most of the material themselves before bringing in the winsome singer du jour to record a vocal track.

They included Sinitta, Rick Astley, Princess, and ex-Australian soap opera stars Kylie Minogue and Jason Donovan. Of them all, only Kylie Minogue achieved any significant success after the label's heyday. The SAW style combined contemporary dance club music with almost offensively bland synthesizers. It proved excruciatingly popular with teens and won a strong following in the gay community even across the Atlantic.

Aitken was a real musician and had earned his crust playing gigs on cruise ships before hitting the big time. Along with Mike Stock, he formed the musical kernel of the hit machine, while Waterman tended more to the business side of things. After a decade of commercial success, and much derision from the musical cognoscenti, the trio broke up in 1991.

Matt Aitken has continued to be involved in things musical and enjoys participating in motor races as a sideline.

WARRIOR MATTHEWS

Matthew Aylmer was born in County Meath, Ireland, and entered the Royal Navy as a lieutenant in 1679. Progressing quickly to the rank of captain, he saw service in the Mediterranean. During the Glorious Revolution, he sided with the rebels and retained his command. In later years, he fought in the wars in which Britain attempted to restrain Louis XIV's expansionist ambitions.

He participated in the Battle of Barfleur, the key naval engagement of the War of the Austrian Succession. The French fleet which was defeated in the engagement, had intended to land an army in Britain to attempt the restoration of James II to the British throne.

Afterwards Aylmer made his reputation with service in North Africa, during which he signed a number of peace treaties with North African principalities. He represented both Portsmouth and Dover in Parliament and was raised to the peerage in 1718 as Lord Aylmer of Balrath.

Matthew Aylmer was promoted to the rank of rear admiral in 1720 and died shortly thereafter. The frigate HMS *Aylmer* was named after Matthew Aylmer, and performed heroic service in World War Two, sinking two German U-boats, including one by ramming.

Matthew Bunker Ridgway (1895-1993) was a US Marine general who led parachute landings over Normandy in World War II and later achieved distinction in the

Korean War when he took charge of the Eighth Army which had been forced into a demoralising retreat after China's shock entry into the war.

He restored the morale of the dispirited UN troops and began a pushback operation which drove the Chinese forces out of South Korean territory.

Ridgway acquired the nickname of "Old Iron Tits" for his habit of hanging grenades from his upper torso.

Matthew Bessarab (also Matei Basarab) was a 17th century ruler of the Romanian province of Wallachia which then was subject to the Ottoman Empire.

Along with his contemporary and fellow Romanian, Basil the Wolf, the ruler of Moldavia, he is credited with introducing enlightened judicial reform to his territory and laying the foundation for the development of Romanian as a literary language by establishing a printing press and issuing books in Romanian, which, until then, had been a spoken language only.

Punishments prescribed in the new Romanian legal code included provisions for rapists to be raped themselves in retribution for their crime – by what or whom is not clear. Seducers had boiling lead poured down their throats; and arsonists were burned alive. Historians tell us that this constituted progress, however, so God knows what must have preceded it.

Paradoxically, given the extremely similar reform initiatives which each pushed through in their respective territories, Matthew Bessarab and Basil the Wolf passionately hated one another.

Their ill-feeling culminated in the clash of arms, with two major battles, each of which Matthew Bessarab won decisively. Following his second defeat, Basil was dethroned and expelled by his own people in 1653, ultimately dying in exile in a Constantinople prison. Matthew Bessarab died in 1654.

MATHEW STREET

Mathew Street in Liverpool is the location of the famous Cavern Club, where the Beatles first made a name for themselves.

The club still exists today and features live music almost every night. The whole surrounding area has been turned into a shrine to the Fab Four, featuring a Beatles shop, a Beatles information centre and a Beatles gallery.

A free Mathew Street music festival is held in August each year.

MORE WARRIOR MATTHEWS

When British and French armies assaulted the Russian port city of Sevastopol during the Crimean War, they found themselves engulfed in bitter siege warfare.

Trench systems and massive artillery bombardments were the order of the day, in many ways prefiguring the kind of fighting which was to dominate the First World War sixty years later.

On April 17th 1855, it was during one of these fierce artillery duels that Captain **Matthew Dixon** earned his Victoria Cross. His unit was struck by a Russian shell which ignited ammunition stores, causing a large explosion which rendered useless all but one of the seven artillery pieces under his command and killed or wounded ten of his men.

Undeterred, and on his own, Matthew doggedly continued firing the one gun which remained operational until darkness set in and help could come.

Matthew came from a distinguished military family. His grandfather had been an admiral and his father was a major-general. In time, too, Matthew rose to the rank of major-general. He died in 1905 at the age of 83.

Named after the American navigation expert, and the son of a distinguished Victorian educationalist, translator and author, **Matthew Fontaine Maury Meiklejohn** was born in 1870. He was educated at the elite Fettes College in Edinburgh and afterwards joined the Gordon Highlanders.

After seeing service in India, he was re-deployed to South Africa to confront the Boers during the Boer War. He earned his Victoria Cross at the battle of Elaandslaagte on 29th October 1899. His unit took heavy losses as it advanced on Boer positions. When his men wavered after a number had been cut down, he stepped forward and continued the advance, rallying his men around him. In the course of the assault, he sustained four grievous injuries but survived.

After the battle he and his men were besieged by the Boers in the town of Ladysmith. There, his injuries were such that his right arm had to be amputated. Some were amazed that he survived at all.

The garrison at Ladysmith was eventually relieved, and Matthew later took on a staff role in the military, rising to the rank of major. His life ended abruptly in 1913 when his horse bolted while he was out riding in Middlesex. Unable to bring it under control, when he saw that it was about to ride through a group of women and children, he turned the horse into some nearby railings, sacrificing his life to save theirs.

Lt. Matthew Croucher was awarded the George Cross for the exceptional gallantry he displayed in Afghanistan on February 9th 2008 when he leapt on a grenade, smothering it with his body to protect his fellow soldiers from danger. Matthew's unit had been investigating a compound where it was believed IEDs (Improvised Explosive Devices) were being produced.

Although the compound unexpectedly proved to be unoccupied, signs of IED production were found there. As the unit was leaving the building, Matthew stumbled over a tripwire, releasing a concealed grenade which now rolled free, presenting a grave danger to everyone present.

In a flash, Matthew decided that the best thing to do was shout a warning to his comrades, then roll onto the grenade, covering it with the heavy rucksack he was carrying, which contained all of the unit's supplies. After bracing himself for the impact, Matthew was surprised to discover that he was still alive, although he said it took him about thirty seconds to be sure of that.

His shredded backpack absorbed most of the impact, meaning that the other members of his unit sustained only minor injuries. Amazingly, Matthew refused medical evacuation after the incident, remaining with his comrades and participating in a firefight not long afterwards, during which he is said to have "neutralised" an enemy fighter.

Thomas Matthews was a British sailor who joined the Royal Navy in 1690 and worked his way up through the ranks to become first a captain, then a squadron commander. After seeing action dealing with pirates off the coast of India, he took a hiatus from the navy in 1724 before rejoining in 1736 and being promoted to the rank of vice-admiral in 1742.

In the War of the Austrian Succession (1740-48), Matthews was involved in an action which generated a great deal of controversy: the blockade of Toulon. Britain was then at war with Spain, and it was expected that France would enter the war on the Spanish side at any moment.

Matthews had therefore been ordered to guard the port of Toulon, where French and Spanish ships were holed up, and to attack them if they emerged. Emerge they soon did, with the French commander under specific instructions to let the British fire first.

Wild winds around the port meant that Matthews was unable to line up his ships correctly, as prescribed by naval doctrine. His difficulties in this were aggravated by a disgruntled subordinate, Richard LeStock, who seemed less than keen to follow his instructions.

In the end, after several days of pursuing the French ships and unsuccessfully attempting to form his line, Matthews decided to attack more haphazardly. The ensuing action was chaotic, and the French ships escaped with only moderate damage.

The Toulon battle became a great public scandal. Matthews resigned immediately, but nonetheless found himself being court-martialled, along with LeStock and numerous lesser commanders.

In the end, Matthews was cashiered and LeStock was exonerated.

Matthew (Matthias) Corvinus is widely considered to be Hungary's greatest ever king. The son of John Hunyadi, who inflicted a crushing defeat on the Ottoman Turks at the Siege of Belgrade in 1456 before dying in the same year, Matthias too was to spend much of his life at war.

Far more than just a warrior, though, Corvinus worked to bring his country out of the Middle Ages and into modernity, inviting foreign scholars to his court, putting the rule of law on a firmer foundation, and assembling a vast library of two thousand volumes which ultimately acquired an almost mythical status within Hungary.

Following Matthias' death in 1490, the library was lost, its volumes either destroyed or dispersed to no one knew where. Hungary itself fell under foreign domination, and the lost library became a symbol of Hungary's vanished glory. The quest to recover it became a national obsession.

The history of Matthias Corvinus is the source of some emotional tension between Hungary and Romania. He was born in Kolozsvar, in Transylvania, which today is part of Romania. There is a statue of him in the city's main square, yet most Romanians have little love for him, regarding him as a Hungarian.

Transylvania itself has long been disputed between the two countries.

The name Corvinus comes from the image on the family crest: the raven. Matthias was also known as the Raven King. Like King Arthur in Britain, and Frederick

Barbarossa in Germany, legends are told of his future re-appearance. It is said that he is not dead, but sleeping, and will return one day in his country's hour of need.

⟫◆⟪

WHAT IS THE MATTHEW EFFECT?

The **Matthew** effect is a kind of snowballing principle according to which people who have a lot of something will get more of it. The name comes from a quote in the Book of Matthew: "to them that hath, more shall be given".

There are illustrations of the principle in a number of separate fields. For example, in the world of academic research, the term "Matthew effect" describes the process by which an already distinguished researcher will get a disproportionate amount of the credit whenever a joint paper is published with other less distinguished researchers.

Sometimes graduate students do all the work and get none of the credit. Nobel prizes have even been awarded on this basis, which, of course, subsequently gave rise to extremely heated disputes.

WHERE IS MATTHEW ISLAND?

Matthew Island is located in the South Pacific, about 300 miles east of New Caledonia. It is a tiny islet, approximately half a kilometre square, although its size actually changes over time because it is highly volcanic and the eruptions can give rise to changes in the landscape when the lava cools and forms into new territory.

The island was first discovered in 1788 by Thomas Gilbert of the Royal Navy who named it after the owner of his ship. No one lives on the island and there is no significant animal or vegetable life there.

Despite its barren nature, however, the island is the subject of a comic opera territorial dispute between France and the former British colony of Vanuatu. France first claimed the island in 1929, and Britain launched a counter-claim on behalf of the New Hebrides in 1965, erecting signs to make the point. France removed the signs in 1975 and put up some of its own.

France has also installed unmanned seismic and weather monitoring stations there. In 1980, Britain's former colony of New Hebrides became the independent nation of Vanuatu and was forced to defend its claim on its own against France. The war of the signs continues. Once every ten years or so, one country removes the other's signs and puts up its own.

Ships from the Vanuatu navy also visit Matthew Island once per year, on Vanuatu's Independence Day, and raise the flag there to assert their claim of sovereignty. The following day, in ritual fashion, France sends a diplomatic protest note to Vanuatu.

———◆———

WOT, NO MATTHEWS?

In some fields, there is a curious lack of Matthews where the popularity of the name and its biblical heritage might have been expected to produce at least a few. For example, there has never been a Pope called Matthew.

There has never been a British, Canadian, Australian or New Zealand Prime Minister or an American President called Matthew. Looking for Matthews of Prime Ministerial calibre, you have to forget about serious countries and go all the way down to Dominica to find one. Step forward, **Matthew Walter**.

But wait. It turns out he wasn't even a real Prime Minister, only an Acting Prime Minister. Sad or what?

In the history of the British Army, there have been over 100 Field Marshals. Not one Matthew among them. Matthews don't seem to have the Right Stuff either. Of the more than 500 human beings who have left planet Earth and ventured into space, not one has been called Matthew.

Out of the more than 1000 Nobel Prize winners, nary a Matthew is to be found. The nearest a Matthew has got to a Nobel Prize is an Ig Nobel prize. These are a kind of comic alternative to the real Nobel prizes (Nobel – Noble – Ignoble, geddit?) awarded to celebrate absurd or useless research.

British scientist **Robert Matthews** won the Ig Nobel for chemistry in 1996 after publishing a paper in a scientific journal investigating the great mystery of why toast always falls on the buttered side.

⟾◆⟸

A Name With Authority

Like his great-grandfather Sigmund, founder of psychoanalysis, **Matthew Freud** also mines the mysteries of the human psyche, but in a more down-to-earth way: he works in public relations. His company, Freud Communications, is one of the most high-profile PR outfits in the UK. Married to Elisabeth Murdoch, daughter of the media tycoon Rupert, his personal life never fails to enjoy a high profile too.

A TRIBUTE FROM MATTHEW

Matthew Henderson was a good friend of the Scottish poet Robert Burns, who wrote a fine poetic tribute to him when he died, extracts from which are quoted below:

He's gane! he's gane! he's frae us torn,
The ae best fellow e'er was born!
Thee, Matthew, Nature's sel' shall mourn
By wood and wild,
Where, haply, pity strays forlorn,
Frae man exil'd!

Mourn him, thou sun, great source of light!
Mourn, empress of the silent night!
And you, ye twinkling starnies bright,
My Matthew mourn!
For through your orbs he's ta'en his flight,
Ne'er to return.

If ony whiggish whingin sot,
To blame poor Matthew dare, man,
May dool and sorrow be his lot!
For Matthew was a rare man.

Every Boy's Dream

Computer engineer **Matthew Atherton** got to live out every child's fantasy – by becoming a superhero! Matthew was the first winner of the television series *Who Wants To Be a Superhero?* in which contestants would compete by putting forward superheroes of their own devising. Matthew's entry was Feedback, who could generate a powerful electrical field around his body and absorb new powers by playing video games! Matthew's prize for winning the series was to see Feedback feature in a comic written by the legendary comic writer Stan Lee and in a film on the Sci-Fi channel.

⟹◆⟸

Multi-talented Matthew

Matthew Buckinger (also Matthias Buchinger) is certainly one of the most curious Matthews who has ever lived. Born in Nuremberg in 1674 without arms, feet or thighs, he nonetheless defied his natural shortcomings to achieve extraordinary things. Although he had no hands, he became skilled in manipulating things with his wrists and the 'fin-like' appendages that protruded from them. In this way, Matthew mastered several musical instruments, even inventing a few of his own, and became a remarkably adept artist. Amazingly, he could also do conjuring tricks, much like a modern stage magician. Matthew used his creative skills to earn a living for himself, offering musical and magical performances and selling portraits he had made. He came to Britain several times and at one point he boasted that he had performed "before three Emperors, and most of the Kings and Princes in Europe, and in particular, several times before his Majesty King George."

Despite his unprepossessing appearance, he proved attractive to women, marrying four wives in the course of his life. And, although he had no arms or legs, at least one of his appendages seemed to be in full working order. Matthew fathered a total of fourteen children.

⟫◆⟪

LITTLE MATT

With his success in the radio-cum-TV show *Little Britain*, **Matt Lucas** has become one of the biggest names in British comedy in recent years. Lucas specialises in playing grotesque characters, something no doubt facilitated by his own rather unusual appearance – bald and curiously childlike, he resembles nothing so much as a grinning super-villain who has just escaped from the set of the latest James Bond film.

Openly gay, Lucas entered a civil partnership with Kevin McGee in 2006, only to break up with him two years later, citing irreconcilable differences. Alongside his comedy work, Lucas has also performed in a number of conventional acting roles on stage and screen.

UNTRUSTWORTHY MATTHEWS

Rogue trader **Matthew Piper** racked up £60 million in losses for his City employer Morgan Stanley before being rumbled in May 2008. The 36-year-old executive was said to have been falsifying the estimated profits on his transactions for some time, possibly to inflate his own bonus payments. Despite the hefty sums involved, Matthew only comes a measly 33rd in the list of all-time rogue-trader miscreants, ranked according to the amount lost.

On the British list, however, he's placed a respectable fourth.

World's Worst Rogue Traders

Name	Amount lost	Country
1. Jerome Kerviel	£3.8 billion	France
2. John Meriwether	£2.76 billion	USA
3. Brian Hunter	£2 billion	USA
4. Yasuo Hamanaka	£1.3 billion	Japan
33. Matthew Piper	£60 million	UK

Worst British Rogue Traders

1. Nick Leeson	£800m
2. Peter Young	£450m
3. Kyriacos Papouis	£80m
4. Matthew Piper	£60m

Matthew Hattabaugh was one of the most enterprising con men of recent times. He set up his own bank in San Francisco called Pacific American Capital Holding Inc. It wasn't a real bank, though. In fact, he was operating it out of his own home – but that didn't stop the deposits rolling in. Matthew managed to bag more than $600,000 in total – and he had millions more on the way – before law enforcement authorities shut him down in 2002. What makes the crime even more interesting is that the victims of the fraud were not ordinary punters – they were professional investment brokers whom Matthew had managed to fool. It's said he had a talent for sounding authoritative, intelligent and knowledgeable. In person, he always wore the smartest suits and looked impeccably swish. In the end, he copped five years in prison for wire fraud.

⟸◆⟹

Not So Tough Matthew?

Matthew 'Mancow' Muller is one of the innumerable right-wing blowhard radio talk-show hosts who infest the airwaves in America. When the Bush administration invaded Iraq, he proclaimed that those who disagreed with the decision ought to be tried for treason. Later, when torture allegations started to circulate, Muller was unmoved. Water-boarding, the American practice of subjecting prisoners to simulated drowning, was not torture, he insisted. To prove it, he offered to undergo it himself. A US Marine was found to administer the 'enhanced interrogation practice', and Muller lasted a whole six seconds ("eight seconds less than the average person") before signalling desperately for it to stop. Badly shaken, he concluded that water-boarding was in fact torture, after all.

There is every chance we have missed a Matthew, or two.

Let us know at **www.stripepublishing.co.uk**

ACKNOWLEDGEMENTS

The mistakes are all mine. The plagiarisms are all someone else's. And the rare, glorious verbal felicities – well, how did they get in there?

And finally, a big thank you to Dan Tester and everyone at Stripe Publishing for giving me the opportunity to write this book.

BIBLIOGRAPHY

Matthew Fontaine Maury: Scientist of the Sea,
Frances Leigh Williams, Rutgers University Press (1963)

A Conspiracy So Immense – The World of Joe McCarthy,
David M. Oshinsky, Oxford University Press (2005)

The Late Medieval Age of Crisis and Renewal, 1300-1500: A Biographical Dictionary,
Clayton J. Drees, Greenwood Press (2001)

Who's Who in Naval History: From 1550 to the Present,
Alastair Wilson and Joseph F. Callo, Routledge (2004)

The Great Admirals: Command at Sea, 1587-1945,
Jack Sweetman, Naval Institute Press (1997)

China in the Sixteenth Century: the Journals of Matthew Ricci, 1583-1610,
Louis J. Gallagher - transltr, Matthew Ricci – author, Random House (1953)

The Balkans: Roumania, Bulgaria, Servia, and Montenegro,
William Miller, G. P. Putnam's Sons (1972)

A Black Explorer at the North Pole,
Matthew A. Henson, University of Nebraska Press (1989)

The Kingdom of Matthias, A Story of Sex and Salvation in 19th-Century America,
Paul E. Johnson and Sean Wilentz, Oxford University Press (1995)

Encyclopedia of Modern Worldwide Extremists and Extremist Groups,
Stephen E. Atkins, Greenwood Press (2004)

Watergate and Afterward: The Legacy of Richard M. Nixon,
Leon Friedman, William F. Levantrosser, Greenwood Press (1992)

A Progression of Judges: A History of the Supreme Court of British Columbia,
David R. Verchere, University of British Columbia Press (1988)

The Spleen and Other Poems,
Matthew Green, T Cadell Jnr and W Davies (1796)

Matthew Prior, Poet and Diplomatist,
Charles Kenneth Eves, Columbia University Press (1939)

A Historical Dictionary of Germany's Weimar Republic, 1918-1933,
C. Paul Vincent, Greenwood Press (1997)

Lost Christianities: The Battle for Scripture and the Faiths We Never Knew,
Bart D. Ehrman, Oxford University Press (2003)

Encyclopaedia Britannica 2008

RECOMMENDED WEBSITES

www.nytimes.com
www.wikipedia.org
www.guardian.co.uk
www.independent.co.uk
www.timesonline.co.uk
www.bbc.co.uk
www.spiegel.de
www.nationalarchives.gov.uk